PRAISE FOR BRAD SMITH

I have to say I'm so grateful to this company and finding Brad Smith. The customer service was amazing and I'm now on my way to getting my credit and life back together.

—Danyell H., Plano, TX

We've had a really tough time with our finances this year. I wasn't at all excited about using a third party to help us, but these guys really came through. We must have had two or three calls with Brad before making the decision. The paperwork was exhausting, but understandable.

We're thankful that Rescue One was able to answer our questions and get us back on track for a better year. Highly recommend!
—Steve W., La Mirada, CA

Rescue One Financial is a great place to get your financial situation back on track. The company's main goal is to provide you with a consolidation loan to pay off your credit cards and other debts and save you tons of money in interest. If for what ever reason you can't qualify for a loan, they also offer debt relief services, but only if you need them. They are truly a great company with an honest staff and will only provide you with options that make the most sense for your situation.

—Tim J., Costa Mesa, CA

Solid system that works!
—Chris Y., Kansas City, MO

I received their letter in the mail and, since I was drowning in debt, I thought I should try them out. I can't believe how fast and helpful Rescue One Financial is. They were polite, explained everything, and were caring. I'm actually able to save and put a little money to the side. Thank you so much!

—Belinda A., Fort Lauderdale, FL

Rescue One Financial and Brad Smith changed my life and allowed me to start all over again. Thank you so much for a new beginning.

—Steve T., Miami, FL

Last year my business partner ditched me and I had a really tough time with my business and personal finances. I was desperately looking for help when suddenly one day I found Rescue One Financial. Brad Smith's advise and service helped me get out my financial crunch and restart my business. They have very nice staff who took care of my situation professionally. I highly recommend them to everyone wanting to get out of debt.

—Neil G., Irvine, CA

LET'S TALK

TALK

ABOUT

DEBT

Bradley W. Smith

LET'S TALK ABOUT DEBT

The Inside Scoop
on Credit, Loans, and
Financial Rescue

Advantage®

Published by Advantage, Charleston, South Carolina.
Member of Advantage Media Group.

ADVANTAGE is a registered trademark, and the Advantage colophon is a trademark of Advantage Media Group, Inc.

Printed in the United States of America.

10 9 8 7 6 5 4 3 2 1

ISBN: 978-1-59932-609-2
LCCN: 2017950302

Book design by Megan Elger.

This publication is designed to provide accurate and authoritative information in regard to the subject matter covered. It is sold with the understanding that the publisher is not engaged in rendering legal, accounting, or other professional services. If legal advice or other expert assistance is required, the services of a competent professional person should be sought.

Advantage Media Group is proud to be a part of the Tree Neutral® program. Tree Neutral offsets the number of trees consumed in the production and printing of this book by taking proactive steps such as planting trees in direct proportion to the number of trees used to print books. To learn more about Tree Neutral, please visit www.treeneutral.com.

Advantage Media Group is a publisher of business, self-improvement, and professional development books. We help entrepreneurs, business leaders, and professionals share their Stories, Passion, and Knowledge to help others Learn & Grow. Do you have a manuscript or book idea that you would like us to consider for publishing? Please visit advantagefamily.com or call 1.866.775.1696.

*This book is dedicated to my late mother, who spent every dime she had
on her kids. It was one hell of a ride, but clearly not recommended.*

*And to my Father who forced me at an early age
to be interested in ALL things financial.*

*And to my wife, Carrie, who gambled every penny
we had on this wild ride, thank you.*

*And to my three boys, who at their age have
no concept of money, keep reading....*

TABLE OF CONTENTS

WHY NOT BANKRUPTCY?

FINDING THE RIGHT HELP

IT PAYS TO SETTLE

A NEW WAY OF LIFE

ACKNOWLEDGMENTS

I am not a self-made man.

Every time I am asked to speak at a conference or by some business professional about what made us successful or what our secret sauce is, I am reminded that I got a lot of help.

First and foremost, I had two great partners in Branden Millstone and Mark Photoglou who, without them, we would not be where we are today. They took calculated risks that I probably would have not. They knew how to build a culture of "work hard, play harder". To them, I am forever grateful to have been in a business that helps people. To Brent Novotchin and John Conzelman, our two owner operators who spent long hours developing our staff and doing the things that needed to be done on a daily basis, I am forever grateful. It is an honor to work with the people that I do on a daily basis.

To every Financial Consultant that has walked through our doors over the years, I thank you for caring enough about people in a financial hardship when most are uninterested. You are the reason that this business is successful.

To every client we have ever touched and to the people, we still seek to help, I have been there several times myself and I can tell you from personal experience, there is a way out. The dark days that you are experiencing today can be wiped out if you have the right strategy.

Thank you to Ditech, a mortgage company here locally in Costa Mesa, CA for firing me when they did. From those dark days, I met my beautiful wife who, without her, I would still be valeting cars somewhere. I love you Carrie and thanks for selling everything we had to make this journey possible.

And finally to the people that bought this book, there will always be moments in life where you will need some outside motivation and assistance, I commend you for taking that first step.

Now turn the page and learn something.

ABOUT THE AUTHOR

Bradley W. Smith, an experienced Financial Advisor, spent years counseling the Ultra High Net Worth population of Los Angeles and Beverly Hills. He soon realized that the game was stacked and larger financial institutions were more concerned with extracting wealth from individuals than they were on building it. After ten years with two of the largest investment banking companies on the planet, he set out to gain an understanding and interworking of the mortgage banking business in what is now looked at as one of the biggest bubbles we have seen in this century. Armed with enough knowledge about lending and credit, he soon ventured in to the Debt Resolution space, something he knew nothing about.

Today, with the guidance and leadership of his partners, he has developed one of the most successful debt management companies in the country. It has been ranked in the top 15 of the Inc. 500, named one of OCBJ's Fastest Growing Companies and also listed as one of the Best Places to Work in Orange County, CA. Rescue One Financial today has helped over 500,000 clients find a better way of life. They have resolved over $6B in unsecured debt for their clients since opening their doors.

Mr. Smith today is an active board member of the AFCC, (American Fair Credit Council) which is the industry watch dog of the Debt Resolution industry. He is also the Treasurer of the Better Business Bureau and has helped that organization to be one of the most successful in the nation.

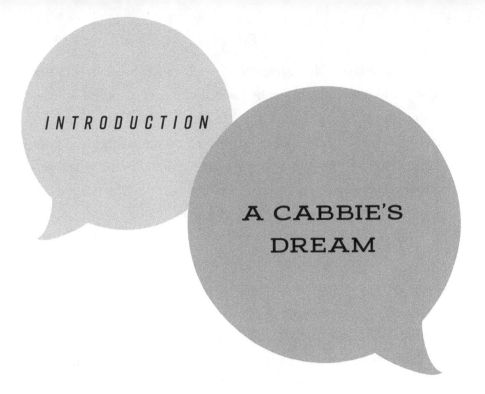

A CABBIE'S DREAM

The taxi driver who picked me up outside the World Trade Center was trolling for tips—but not the usual kind.

"So, you're one of those finance guys?" he asked me. I got the impression he asked a lot of his fares that question. It turned out he was a day trader of Internet stocks, dreaming of the day he would not be sitting behind that wheel. He was sure he could make it big.

This was in the late 1990s, in the latter days of the dot-com boom. At the time, I worked for Morgan Stanley and was involved in numerous initial public offerings. An analyst's strong buy recommendation in those days could send a stock soaring by 200 or 300 percent in the course of a single day. Internet companies had no real earnings basis—in fact, one of the criteria for valuing a tech company's stock was how many "eyeballs," or hits, its website received.

As the cabbie clipped through the intersections, he pumped me for advice on anything I might know that could give him an edge in the market. He boasted about how much he made as a day trader—and it was a lot more, he assured me, than he pulled in from cruising the streets. This was a giddy time for Wall Street, and by virtue of my employment there—I worked on the eighty-third floor of Tower two—I found that people often would ask me my opinion on financial matters.

Just how long can this last? I asked myself as I stepped out of the cab. And of course, the tech bubble was soon to burst. As for that taxi driver, I suspect that the high-flying and quick-diving economy sooner or later conspired to burst his bubble, as well. He seemed to me to be a symbol of what Alan Greenspan, the Federal Reserve chairman at the time, called the "irrational exuberance" of those days.

There were four or five years, from about 1995 to the turn of the millennium, in which one could make money in the stock market with almost unprecedented ease. The S&P 500 index rose nearly 140 percent over that time frame—and went up almost 40 percent in one year alone. It was almost as if you could choose your securities by throwing darts at the stock listings in the Wall Street Journal, and no matter where they landed, you would come across as a brilliant investor.

I often got calls from clients who had seen the investment flavor of the day on CNBC or some other media report. They had no idea what the company did, but they saw that its stock was going up fifteen or twenty points a day, and they wanted in on the action. If they were engaging in any sort of analysis at all, it was highly amateurish, but they were making money nonetheless at day trading.

The phone calls would pour in to my desk as people sought my perspective, and I would look for the fundamentals—but there really were no fundamentals to be seen. These were companies that were reporting losses and were operating on money from a variety of investment banks and early-stage funding rounds.

It was an exciting time, but it was absurd. We all learned, many of us the hard way, that time of wheeling and dealing had to end. In the wake of it all, people were left with mountains of debt. Times had seemed to be so good for so long that people loaded themselves up with what appeared to be an inexhaustible supply of credit. They were to learn that nothing is forever.

WHEN THINGS TURNED UGLY

Soon I left Morgan Stanley and, with a friend who made me an offer I couldn't refuse, I started my own money-management firm in Southern California. We managed about $100 million of other people's money. The market was so robust and it was so easy to make money for people that a colleague and I decided we could do this on our own, without Morgan Stanley or Merrill Lynch or anyone behind us. I was in my late twenties, and I had a false sense of reality.

It was about eight months before the collapse that we started our office in Irvine, building to about thirty people. We also set up an office in the Brentwood neighborhood of Los Angeles. My partner managed the aggressive side of the portfolio, and I managed the conservative, long-term blue chips. A client might come to us with an 80/20 mix of conservative versus speculative investments, and my partner did so well for them that they were moving most of their money toward his end of the portfolio.

As a result, our clients took a major hit when the economy soured, and it happened within a matter of months. The NASDAQ plunged. As you can imagine, it was difficult to get new clients. People who were heavily into the market found their portfolios down by 40 or 50 percent, so not much new money was flowing in. I managed to get out of that gig with no issues or lawsuits.

I joined another firm and spent another several months in the business, but I was well on my way to exiting the industry. Never had there been so many brokers as in the days before the fall, and when the bubble finally burst, they left in droves. People were petrified at that point.

It often was the degree of leverage that did investors in. People were borrowing on margin to buy more stock than they could afford. The arrangement was unsuitable for them. They ended up deeply in debt, and a lot of that debt went on credit cards.

The baby boom generation had invested heavily in that boisterous market, and when boomers pulled out, they looked for somewhere else to put their money—and it went into the real estate market. It was as if we began moving from one bubble to the next, from the tech bubble to the mortgage bubble.

We traded the stock euphoria for the mortgage euphoria. People were getting loans without much in the way of documentation of income or employment. Once the easy money in the mortgage market was gone, people again were left with massive amounts of unsecured personal and credit card debt.

CAUGHT IN THE TRAP OF DEBT

It's human nature to chase the good times. People go after the money. They favor whatever happens to be the fad of the day, and they get themselves in trouble that way. What I do now is help people find their way out of trouble. Many people today are hurting, loaded with debt, and they don't know where to turn. They may fear bankruptcy. They do, however, have alternatives, as I will explain in the pages ahead.

Today, I operate a company called Rescue One Financial. We help struggling consumers negotiate fair settlements and meet their current debt obligations, and we also help them understand how they got into financial trouble in the first place and how to avoid debt in the future.

Although I also help businesses, this book focuses on "the little guy," and anyone caught in the trap of debt who needs to know the best steps. Most people don't know that they have other options than bankruptcy.

After I tell clients about their alternatives, they often tell me they will first consult with their financial advisor. I can tell you from experience that most financial advisors don't know anything about this type of program. They are trained to deal with people who have substantial net worth. They don't know what to do with people who lack money, are highly leveraged, or are facing bankruptcy.

I have seen so much in my career that has made me want to help people in a much different way than I once did. The investment banks are focused on products and profits and want each of their advisors to bring in the money. I saw how the companies rolled out the products and how certain stocks got an upgrade because of an investment banking relationship. I didn't always feel that what was suggested for the client was in the client's best interest.

Later, when I worked in the mortgage industry, I dealt with some loan products that could get consumers into deep trouble, such as the "2-28" or the "3-27," which are thirty-year loans that are locked in only for the first two or three years before adjusting to what could be a terrible rate that the consumer simply can't afford. It was the loan often given to subprime borrowers. They got a brief break of a few years with lower monthly payments, and then, when the rate adjustment came along, they were in trouble.

The banks and Wall Street were not looking out for the best interests of homeowners. With property values soaring and interest rates dropping rapidly, many borrowers wanted to refinance. They could shop for a new loan to pay off their old one and also to pull out some cash, often with no increase in the monthly payment. They often faced a prepayment penalty on the old loan, however, which in effect locked them into the existing deal.

A similar thing happened with what the mortgage industry called "the neg-am loan"—a negatively amortized loan where your minimum monthly payment doesn't even cover the interest-only portion of your monthly payment. With a neg-am loan, you may have a really low monthly payment, but the actual balance on your loan is increasing each month. In an environment where homes are going up 15 to 20 percent a year, it isn't a big deal. But in a market that is flat to down, it is a very big deal, because the homeowner gets trapped in that home without an opportunity to refinance. And those loans, too, had a feature where the interest rates would reset after three or five years, leaving the homeowner in a terrible position financially.

In those days I felt as if I might be part of the problem, both when I was working in the investment banking industry and when I moved on to the mortgage industry and saw those kind of loans. I had experienced two big bubbles, and when the second one popped, I wondered, "Where are we headed next?"

A LOOK IN THE MIRROR

After looking at so many credit reports, I saw that people were using their homes as ATMs. They were making more money in the appreciation of their homes than they were on their jobs. It wasn't uncommon to see $50,000 to $70,000 of credit card debt on a borrower's credit report. How to deal with it seemed like a no-brainer. They figured they could just pay off the debt with a refinance, run the credit cards up again, and do it all over in a few years.

I had to look at myself in the mirror. I think that's really what got me into my business today of helping people get out of debt. *Will I be part of the problem*, I asked myself, *or will I be part of the solution?*

CHAPTER 1

OFF THE TREADMILL

O nce, it was common practice to send people to debtors' prison when they could not pay their obligations. In places such as the infamous Fleet Prison in London, inmates were forced to spend hours on the "treadmill," on which they would labor to no avail. Sometimes the treadmills were used as power for a gristmill, but more often the wheels turned for no purpose. To work hard and accomplish nothing has long been considered a severe punishment.

Many people still feel imprisoned by debt, and they still feel as if they are on a treadmill (although today they manage to maintain their freedom, at least physically). To be deeply in debt and unable to see how you will escape can indeed feel as if you are spinning the wheels for nothing.

Even without the threat of imprisonment, people worry deeply about their debts, not understanding what options they might have. Many people wonder what would happen if they were to rack up all their credit cards to the maximum and then not be able to make the payments. Would someone come around to seize all their possessions? Could they be thrown into jail?

Part of the problem has been a collection-agency process that historically has had little regulation. Collection agencies buy portfolios of accounts for eight to ten cents on the dollar, and then they try to get the consumers to cough up as close to 100 percent of that money as possible. It's a very profitable business, but it can also be shady. Collection agents may threaten to contact employers, get the debtor thrown into jail, or send the sheriff to the house. We've heard it all.

My company does not operate that way. Instead, consumers come to us because they know they have an issue. Meanwhile, collection agencies come to us because they know we have the borrower's ear. We serve as an intermediary. Basically, we are saying, "Let's make a deal." We work with the client to set aside money every month, and then we work out an arrangement with the creditor for a settlement.

CAUTION IN TIMES OF STRESS

Almost every day, one of my financial consultants will tell me about someone who called in tears after talking to a collector. The stress can be excruciating, but people need to deal with it effectively. The ostrich approach doesn't work. It's far better to acknowledge your role and say, "Well, I did get myself into this debt, so now I need to do something about it."

The first step for people is to recognize that there is a problem. Once they are at that point, they will be able to listen to their options and decide what would be most suitable and make the most sense for their specific situation.

This calls for caution. A lot of people who claim to be on the side of the consumer are not out to help them at all. They don't want to better the situation. Instead, their game is to make money and gain profits.

You can get into trouble when you listen to people who have an ulterior motive and that motive is not, first and foremost, to keep you out of trouble. When you are under a great deal of stress, you are at risk of jumping for the money. You may pursue a questionable strategy, such as trying to use your house as a credit card. Thinking that way became a way of life for many people while the housing market seemed destined to rise forever. As we have seen, that was not to be the case.

A lot of the problem goes back to the credit-card-issuing companies themselves—the big guys, who play the game of putting people on lifetime repayment plans. That, too, sets people up to fail. It was only a few years ago that credit card companies were first required by law to clearly notify consumers on monthly statements how much they would pay in total if they continued to make only the monthly payment—and how many years it would take to pay off the debt.

Many people had no idea. They figured they would be able to pay off the card the next year, or the year after, or that things would get better. Nobody ever told them that making only the minimum monthly payments would take them decades to erase, say, $15,000 in credit card debt—and at a total cost that could be many times the amount they originally charged.

The regulation requiring that disclosure led to considerable change in the industry. People don't realize how much the daily compounding interest impacts their debt. They simply look at the minimum monthly payment and tell themselves, "Okay, I can afford that." I think the credit card companies have done the American people a huge injustice by putting them in these kinds of situations.

If the credit card companies simply charged the simple interest rate, compounded monthly, in which your minimum monthly payment went partly to the principal and partly to the interest, people would be much better off. But that is not what those companies do. You can be sure that they fought the new regulation. Somehow, they didn't consider it to be in their best interest for that knowledge to get out there.

The lending industry certainly has given people good reason to proceed with caution.

As for the world of the stockbroker, anyone who has seen the movie *The Wolf of Wall Street* has caught a glimpse of it. I experienced that world when I was in college, at the University of Southern California in Los Angeles, and working at a large brokerage house, and I must say that although there are many honorable and professional stockbrokers, there have been some who are not far afield from the portrayal in that movie. Again, caution is in order.

I made four hundred phone calls a day in my college job. I started on the East Coast in the morning and worked my way across to the West Coast. I found myself calling doctors out of surgery and talking rudely to secretaries and other gatekeepers. I'm not proud to have been part of that world, but I was a kid still in college, and I didn't know any better. The best I can say is that I gained an understanding of how that world can work.

I had a Rolodex on which was listed all the rebuttals that somebody possibly could come up with—"I want to talk to my wife," or "I can't talk at work right now," or "I just don't have enough liquid money available right now." Whatever they told me, I would just flip the Rolodex to the corresponding card and read, verbatim, the response most likely to undermine their excuse. It was like a game in which we were told that if we could just get through three of those cards, the odds were that we would sell someone something by the time we got to the fourth.

Obviously, it worked, because people were making lots of money. But it was not very glamorous. When people hear that you work on Wall Street or for a financial service, they think you must be bright; they think it's a glamorous job. They are wrong.

HELPING, NOT HURTING

The lesson, in short, is this: Many of the people in the banking and financial services industries are primarily trying to help themselves. You don't need to look very far before you can find examples of how people are set up to fail. Particularly in the credit card industry, the goal is to keep people in a position of constant debt.

I don't mind telling people that I had a taste of those other worlds when I was very young, because I do something entirely different now. I am not helping people get into trouble. I am helping them get out of trouble. I think I gained a perspective that allowed me—actually, compelled me—to move on. I wised up very quickly to what I was doing to people.

Once, I worked with people of substantial net worth. Now, I work with the little guys and with the people to whom they owe money, striving to get everyone working together to get matters resolved. What I do today is help people get out of debt and show them how to stay out.

Although I do make money in the process, I do so only when I am able to significantly improve someone's situation. I make money by helping people, by getting them out of their mess—otherwise,

I don't make money. It is all performance based. If I don't change someone's situation for the better, if I don't produce results, then I don't get paid. We don't charge anything upfront.

AMID THE MORTGAGE MESS

My time in the mortgage industry seemed more like a job, not a career. I got into that business because I thought I could make some good money. I was not passionate about it. I had never really thought of the mortgage business as anything but the bubble that it was. I figured it would just be a brief stop on the way to doing something else—and yet, I spent several years in that industry, eventually launching my own mortgage brokerage firm.

At the time of the mortgage meltdown, we had been advertising with a nationwide infomercial. We were offering one of those highly aggressive loans—a forty-year loan for $1 million, fixed at 1 percent for the first five years. Those initial payments would be just a few thousand dollars a month. The phones rang off the hook. We would run that five-minute infomercial six times during a thirty-minute time frame. We bought air time all over the United States.

When the end was imminent, banks and investors didn't waste much time backing out of those loans. I recall at one point, over just a few hours, the two or three main investors who ran this type of loan program all decided they no longer wanted to offer it. As we watched those investors back away from the loan, I realized that the end was going to come pretty quickly. It came for the mortgage business within sixty to ninety days.

And yet, the phones still were ringing. We still had our people taking in applications. I remember sitting back in my chair and wondering how all that was going to play out. It felt very much like the moment with the cabbie back at the World Trade Center.

Over three or four years, I had looked at perhaps twenty-five thousand credit reports. *This is crazy,* I thought, *and it can't possibly end well. What is my best move here?* I could see the tremendous amount of debt that people were carrying, but I couldn't see how they would be able to untangle themselves from it. Up until then, the mortgage market had allowed them to either refinance their homes or take a second mortgage to pay off their debts. Now those options were drying up. *This is going to get ugly,* I thought.

A NEW BEGINNING

That is when I started to look into the business of helping people deal with their debts. That was in 2005. We launched Rescue One Financial in 2007 with three partners, and those three were our original salespeople. They would talk to folks on the phone, assess their situations, and try to enroll them in the best program that we could find. We started in a tiny office, eventually ramping up to a staff of a dozen or so, and today we employ more than a hundred financial consultants.

It was a difficult transition for me. Until then, I had dealt with people of high net worth. They had a lot of money and were particular about their credit. And, in the mortgage business, to get the best loan possible you had to have the highest credit score possible. Now, I was dealing with a clientele that was throwing their hands up in frustration over what had become of their credit rating.

For so long, the prevailing presumption was that good people paid their bills, and if you paid on time, you would have good credit, and if you didn't, you would have bad credit, and that made you a bad person. And yet, things got to the point that so many people were so highly leveraged that it was just a matter of time before they were going to start running late on their payments. A tide of bad credit was rolling in, and people were starting to consider their options.

To deal with this, we looked at the different types of plans that we could offer people. In the debt resolution and management space, there are only a few alternatives. One, of course, is bankruptcy, whether it's Chapter 7 (liquidation) or Chapter 13 (rehabilitation). Another is consumer-credit counseling, in which you still pay back 100 percent of what you owe, but you do so at a much lower interest rate, which has less of an impact on your credit score.

Debt settlement was an area that I had heard little about. Because I had done mortgages, I was familiar with consumer-credit counseling, but not with debt settlement. Consumers who are unable to make their minimum monthly payments started to default on their loans and then enroll with us to set money aside. We negotiate with each of the creditors for a settlement, usually around fifty cents on the dollar.

It became a popular approach. We did a lot of marketing online, and we did a lot of direct mail. We became increasingly busy, but it was bittersweet, because we were hearing so many sad stories. People sometimes get into debt because of terrible situations such as the illness or injury of a child when the family has no health insurance. It tugs at you. You want to do anything you can to help people like that.

In many cases, we found that members of the baby boom generation were unwilling to default on any type of credit card. They would fight tooth and nail to keep up. In their upbringing, bankruptcy was something they would never consider. In conversations with them, time and time again we heard, "Hey, I got myself into this, and I owe this money. I'm going to pay back 100 percent of it. I don't know how, but I will do it." I admired that attitude, as that was part of my upbringing as well.

In our business today, we also issue debt consolidation loans for people who have excellent credit. It's similar to what I did in the financial advisory business. It comes down to suitability. We take a look at people's credit, and we go through a budget. We look at their debts and their employment history. From there, we can make the determination as to which is the best option for them. If we are dealing with a business owner, or someone who needs security clearance, or someone whose livelihood would be impacted if they were to enter a program, then that is obviously not the approach we would take.

Right now, we do just shy of a thousand loans per month, and we have found that segment of our business is increasing. These are all unsecured loans. They're almost entirely used for debt consolidation. Once in a while we'll issue loans for other purposes, but for the most part, when people find us, they are interested in their options for dealing with debt.

I may be able to give such clients a new loan on a three- or five-year term at simple interest and at a fixed rate so that they know exactly what to expect. In many cases, in doing that, we're paying off credit card debt that is at a higher interest rate, and we are giving them a better rate. We are saving them money right off the bat on a monthly basis because this is simple, not compounded, interest.

From there, we do our best to counsel them about how to avoid getting into the same situation again. "You did this once," we say, "and they're going to hit you up again. There's no question. It's up to you as to whether you can stay the course and not get yourself into this situation again." We want to set people straight. We want them to move on. The last thing in the world we want are *repeat* customers.

A PLACE FOR COMPASSION

It is true that many people got into trouble because they were riding the tide of a strong economy and thought the good times would never end. Other people, however, got into trouble because of the challenges, sometimes tragic ones, that life put in their path. They need a new start. All manner of things can go wrong that call for compassion in dealing with people.

I saw the other side of the lending business, and I didn't like it—but I understand it. When you owe people money, they expect you to repay it. Lenders expect borrowers to keep their promises. Because I thoroughly understand the business, I can help people who must deal with those lenders as they work out a way to make right on their debts.

I feel that passion plays a major role in anyone's success. It's hard to do well in a business or in a career if you aren't passionate about it. As I learned more about the debt management and settlement business, and gained a deeper understanding of what people were going through, I found it to be a much more meaningful endeavor than showing some wealthy guy how to get a 22 percent return on his portfolio. *This is changing lives*, I thought.

I had not felt that way about any work I had done before. I found myself keeping every testimonial from clients expressing their appreciation for what we had done for them. My representatives and I regularly share emails from people telling us how happy they are that they found us, that we had changed their lives. This work is far more rewarding than anything I have ever done.

CHAPTER 2

BOOMERS AND BUBBLES

I n the roaring nineties, several years before the bursting of the dot-com bubble, I worked in the Merrill Lynch office in affluent Beverly Hills. We were right off Rodeo Drive, and we often had walk-in clientele who would come in and ask questions. The focus of the business was people with high net worth.

As a financial advisor, my job at the time was to work with officers and directors of publicly traded companies who had virtually all their net worth invested in their company's stock. These were people with very specific issues. If your portfolio is tied up in one position, your net worth can fluctuate wildly on a daily basis. Despite the market risk they face, such executives often also face strict controls on how they handle their stock, to protect against inside trading. My job was to help them monetize some of their position with strategies that would help them to diversify. That, at the time, was my forte.

I was new to the business, and only twenty-two years old, straight out of college. I felt awkward at times as a young guy with $40,000 in student loans who was advising people who had a seven-figure net worth on what to do with their money. It is rare that Merrill Lynch would hire people straight out of college. They generally wanted people with a previous career and a Rolodex of contacts to help build the business. I got in, I believe, because I was a good salesperson and had shown that I could develop a business relationship strictly by cold calling—although the company much preferred growing business by referral and word of mouth.

I went through the Merrill Lynch training program, and those two years were my first exposure, other than the cold calling that I did in college, to a real money-management firm. This was much different than what I had experienced at the brokerage firm where I worked during college. There, the "stock jockeys," as the salespeople were known, were much more interested in the aggressive, speculative side of people's portfolios. They sought bigger and bigger transactions but gave no thought to building portfolios or developing financial plans.

Merrill Lynch, by contrast, was very focused at the time on the planning aspects. We could sit down with the client and say, "Okay, these are your goals for where you want to be, and this is where you are now." In many cases, I didn't just get a small piece of the client's overall portfolio, but instead got quite a lot of it, because it all tied together. I would be doing an insurance component and a stock or mutual fund portfolio, and perhaps accounts for the children, such as college funds, etc. I enjoyed that type of work.

The company did things differently than most others. Back then, everyone referred to it as "Mother Merrill," because it was the biggest in the industry, with probably twice as many advisors as any of the others. It was an accelerated and difficult training program. Within the two-year time frame, trainees needed to bring on a thousand new clients and have roughly $10 million under management. The market was not as frothy in the mid-1990s as it became a few years later; my job was a little harder because the stocks were not just going straight up.

Despite my youth, I had a good knowledge of how the markets worked. I developed most of my client base over the phone. Clients who came in off the street seemed to think of me as a kid, but over the phone I believe I came across as older. As long as my performance met their expectations, people trusted me.

From Merrill Lynch in Beverly Hills, I moved on to a job at Morgan Stanley in the World Trade Center. I thought I was brilliant when I left Morgan Stanley to start my own money management firm, thinking that I didn't need all that research behind me and that I could do it on my own. That is when the dot-com bubble collapsed and people started coming back to reality. I was right in the thick of it.

A BLOW TO THE EGO

My entrance into the mortgage industry was with a West Coast company called DiTech, which occupied fifteen floors in a high rise. It was owned by GMAC Mortgage, the financing arm of General Motors. It was an amazing set-up, with four hundred loan officers and four hundred processors, and GM threw hundreds of millions of dollars into the marketing. The company was running ads far and wide. We were told that somewhere on the planet, a DiTech ad was being run once every seven minutes.

Every time a salesperson hung up the phone, it would instantly ring again with another lead. Rates were coming down aggressively, and it seemed that everyone was refinancing. It was not unusual for a loan officer to handle fifty to seventy-five loans a month. It was our job to prequalify people for those loans, run their credit, look at their situation, and lock in their rate before passing the application over to a processor, who did most of the remaining work.

The company would hold mass interviews every few months, bring in dozens of new hires, and then draw a line in the sand. Those who failed to meet that performance line would be fired, and the company would immediately bring in new blood. My first interview was done jointly with forty other people. It was with a manager who had hired and fired more people than anyone else in the history of the company. I ended up on his team.

The office was open twenty-four hours a day, seven days a week. People would come in at six in the morning and work until midnight. They were sleeping in their cars and showering at the gym. We could work as much as we wanted, but on our time cards we had to indicate working forty hours. But if you only worked forty hours in that job, you wouldn't last long. We were required to burn the midnight oil.

I had never experienced such an atmosphere at such a large company, and I recall thinking that the conditions would eventually lead to unhappy employees suing the company. And indeed, a number of years later the company faced a lawsuit claiming unpaid overtime.

I had some success there, and I guess I got a bit arrogant. I was there for about nine months, and near the end of that time I started to work out in the middle of the day or go out to play tennis for a few hours before coming back in to resume work. I figured that I was such a good salesperson, I could spare that time.

One day in 2002, I got a call from Human Resources: "Come on down. We need to talk to you in the conference room." I asked if I should bring my keys and belongings, and the answer was yes. I was handed my final paycheck, which was $14,685, and bid farewell: "Sorry, you didn't make it."

It was a blow to my ego. I had felt invincible with all that Wall Street experience and a pretty good resume. It had been hard for me to get out of the financial advisory business, which I had long felt would be my career path. Ever since my sophomore year in college, I had felt certain that economics was the way I was headed, and I would somehow be in the world of business. I kept abreast of Wall Street happenings and read the Wall Street Journal every day. My focus was on that world.

But when the NASDAQ plunged and all the clients at our money management firm ran for the hills, it seemed as if all that was taken from me. And when I took the job at DiTech just to make money and not to pursue my career, it felt like a step backward—and then to get fired from that job was a loud wake-up call. It took me some time to get over that. I was single and living in Newport Beach at the time, and some days it felt like a struggle just to get up and get dressed and go out to look for a job. I blew through all my savings. It was a dark time for me.

After a few months, however, I picked myself back up and said, "Okay, rates are still low, and the mortgage industry is still very hot." I knew a lot of people who were making good money doing loans, and some of them had recently been waiting tables—and so I jumped back in.

A NEW PERSPECTIVE ON DEBT

For a short while, I worked at a firm that specialized in second mortgages. The majority of those second mortgages were used to pay off credit card debt. The company was doing all direct mail. I would get eight or twelve Internet applications every day.

I looked at these people's budgets and how much credit card debt they had. That was where I first gained a perspective on how much debt was out there. At DiTech, I had been dealing with the A-paper crowd. People with great credit typically don't have a lot of debt. Now, I had taken a dive into the subprime credit space. I saw how leveraged these applicants were, and during my nine months there I looked for a business opportunity of my own.

That's when I started my own mortgage brokerage firm and started hiring people and advertising with the nationwide infomercial. We built that up very quickly, in about two years' time, to about forty people. Times were good. I felt as if I were back. At this point, I was no longer on the phone; I was a manager. I was helping people out with their files. I was the guy in charge. I had one other partner at the time, and we were 50/50 on the deal. I paid off all my student loans. I was in the black.

And when that began to unravel, just a few years into the new millennium, it happened quickly.

I tried to do everything I could to keep the doors open. I went into quite a bit of debt trying to do that without putting myself in too bad of a position. It became clear to us that this mortgage ride was going to be over for a while.

All the banks backed away from the industry. The big banks that had been doing loans ceased to do so. They didn't want any part of it. The guidelines got so tight that you would be lucky to get ten leads on a daily basis, and then you couldn't even close. Maybe one of them would qualify, but then the appraisal would come in too low because values were going down so quickly. When the end came, it came abruptly. So many people working in the industry were left out in the cold. Once that spigot was turned off, they didn't have a lot of options.

I had spent three or four years in the mortgage business, looking at credit reports. The amount of debt that people were carrying was staggering. People filled out applications, and if they had not been late on any payments, the deal was approved. It was nuts back then. At that point, the lenders were looking clearly at credit score and not so much at ability to repay. They said, "Okay, this guy has had credit for three years and has never been late. We'll call that a good risk." They didn't consider the fact that he made $7 or $8 an hour. We used to see that often. Nobody was all that concerned with how much money you made.

Fortunately, I found this industry in which we can help people deal with their debt. I had gone from the burst of the high-tech bubble to the burst of the mortgage bubble, and I had found a new career path that I found highly satisfying. I had found a way to be of genuine assistance.

GOODBYE TO WISHFUL THINKING

I believe some of the blame must go to the credit card companies. They figured that times were good and people would refinance their debt, but it got to the point where there was no way that some of those debts would be repaid. We saw that time and time again. A borrower might earn only $30,000 at their job but figure they could rack up $50,000 in debt each year and just refinance the house as it goes up 20 percent in value, and people indeed might have done that for a number of years, but of course it doesn't always work that way.

I had that talk with people numerous times, and yet they kept coming back. Many of them were baby boomers, but actually it was everyone. So many people were living high on the hog at that point, and they saw their $500,000 home become a $900,000 one within a few years. People believed that those numbers could be real. They believed that they were brilliant and that they had chosen just the right home at just the right time and in just the right place. And sometimes they did, although there was a lot of wishful thinking involved.

We moved from one bubble to the next, and people were left with a mountain of debt. The real estate market let people down, and now many are worried about what happens next. This is a time of grand de-leveraging. Everyone had their car loans and their credit cards and their multiple loans against their house to pay for it all. And then the banks stepped away, saying, "We are out of here, so good luck with that." The American public was looking to get out of debt in any way possible—hopefully without having to file for bankruptcy.

I lived those years, too. I understand how people got into those situations. I had a front-row seat on what was happening in the worlds of Wall Street and lending and real estate, and I have turned my attention to helping people navigate the difficulties in which they now find themselves.

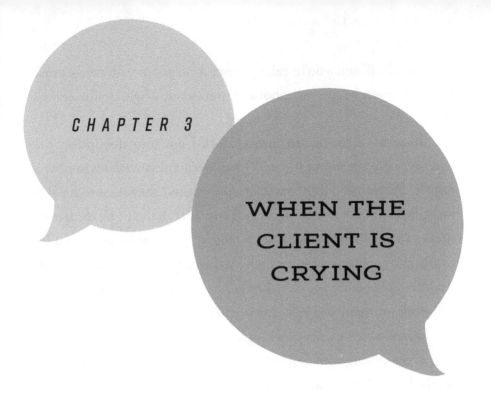

CHAPTER 3

WHEN THE CLIENT IS CRYING

Talking with people when they are in the grips of stress is the hardest thing that we do. I can see that, in many cases, their dire situation is not their fault. Although it's one thing to pile up a load of debt on things you don't really need—people need to exercise some restraint and take responsibility—some of the causes of debt are truly heart wrenching.

Often it is our financial consultants who take the calls at our firm who tell me the stories. This happens regularly. We hear a lot of pain and anguish over the phone and across the desk. It deeply affects our people. They empathize with the clients. In fact, some of our consultants have, at some point, been in the shoes of those who are calling—they have either filed for bankruptcy or gone through a program such as ours.

That's why they can tell the caller, in all sincerity, "Hey, listen, I know that you're in total darkness right now. Maybe your power just got turned off and you're calling from a neighbor's phone because you don't even have a cell phone. Listen, there's light at the end of the tunnel."

There are a lot of unknowns. Until I got into this industry, I had never even heard of it—and I had been a financial advisor for a decade. People need to know their options, and they need to hit this thing head on. It's not going to go away. It truly helps for people to speak to someone who has been through it, who has been in a similar situation of onerous debt, and who has emerged just fine. That does wonders in boosting people's confidence about whether our program will work for them and just how it will operate.

Sometimes we encounter situations where people are in such dire straits through no fault of their own that we want to see them get the break they so sorely need. It can be tough on our team. I don't want them to become numb to the suffering. I don't want them to get to the point where they just deliver some standard pitch to the client. Sometimes I suggest they just get out of the office, go to the gym, go for a walk, or go do something else and get their minds off this for an hour or two.

When you are taking a couple hundred of these phone calls a month, you can tend to get jaded. Every time that phone rings, you know that it is probably a serious situation. That is what it must feel like to be a 911 operator. Our business is not a matter of life or death, but nonetheless we are dealing with people in a very troubled state, and so it is very important for people to take a couple of deep breaths and walk away from it from time to time.

The bright side is this: After handling so many situations, our people get to the point where they have seen it all and are in a good position to help people. They can say: "Listen, I understand, I get it—and these are your options in a situation like this."

HOPING FOR A BREAK

I know personally how it feels. I came very close to needing the sort of services that my business now offers to others. When I was starting the business in 2005, I had racked up almost $60,000 in credit card debt. My wife and I were liquidating our 401(k) and paying rent on our credit card. We were maxed out to the point where banks would not give us any more money.

I was all in: Either this business was going to work, or I would be filing for bankruptcy myself, or looking for some other avenue of settlement. Bankruptcy would have been more likely. Since I was self-employed, I don't think I would have been a candidate for debt management, for which you need a job or income to enroll.

We ended up borrowing $10,000 from her folks and $10,000 from my dad, which is something I never would have thought I would be doing. My father has long worked in the corporate world as a chief financial officer, and he is very conservative. It was an unwritten rule that you didn't do business with family. In the years when I was a stockbroker, no one in the family did any business with me.

When I did approach him, I was prepared with an Excel spreadsheet that projected the first year or two of our business. I carried that printout in my back pocket for months. We were at a restaurant, and I pulled out that dog-eared document. "Here's where we are, and we're just about to turn the corner, just one more month. By the fourteenth month, we will be doing really well."

"I'll give you a loan," he told me, "but you're going to pay me interest on it." It was at the market rate. He had me sign a promissory note, and I think he was the first person I paid back when we were making money.

I never needed to enroll in a program or declare bankruptcy. Still, I wish to share how I felt in those difficult times. I know what it is like to feel that you are just about to turn the corner but worrying you won't get there and hoping someone will give you a break.

WRACKED WITH WORRIES

Sometimes when people find themselves in difficult situations, they hesitate to reach out for help. They may fear that if they reveal what they are going through, somebody will take advantage of them. They suspect there are people out there ready and waiting to pounce.

Actually, it's an understandable attitude. Our industry is not all that well known, and people tend to look for the catch when someone tells them, "I see that you have $100,000 in debt, and I think we can settle that for about half and get you out of debt in three or four years." It seems too good to be true. People worry that it is a scam, or that it doesn't really work, or that they will end up getting sued and end up in bankruptcy anyway.

And if they do go into bankruptcy, they fear they are leaving a record that will haunt them forever, marked as a miscreant who fails to keep promises. That prospect plays on their conscience. Many people have a conditioned belief that if they have poor credit, or if they don't always pay their bills on time, they are somehow a bad person. They may harbor that attitude even if these things happen through no fault of their own, which, as we have seen, may well be the case. They often feel morally responsible and embarrassed.

Making matters worse is that collection agencies often do their utmost to make people feel that way. They find ways to reinforce the impression that only bad people take money from others and don't pay it back. Technology has made it easy to automate the dialing, and in many cases the creditors have the numbers for people's home phones, work phones, and cell phones. The dialing can begin at 8 o'clock in the morning and continue into the evening. Just one creditor can cause a lot of disruption. Imagine if there were eight of them.

HERE TO HELP

You can see why people in debt would hesitate to talk to one more person about their situation. It doesn't seem like anyone wants to cut them a break. When people do call us for help, we help to ease their doubts by explaining that we are performance based and that we don't get paid unless we actually do what we say we will do.

In a way, we are acting as an extended arm of the collection agency, but we truly have the ear of the borrower. We will never treat people badly or make them feel at fault. Even if their decisions have been less than wise, we emphasize that we are here to help.

We never make cold calls. The person in debt comes to us, not vice versa. People need to actively seek the help we offer by responding to a mailing or an Internet notice. That is usually the first step. If we were to chase people, we would be in the same league as the collection agencies. That is not how we do business. Instead, people seek us out as a potential solution, and they soon feel the reassurance to move forward.

When they do come to us, they generally have a variety of questions and are still wondering whether we are legitimate. We feel a lot of satisfaction in revealing the truth to them: all is not lost—there's a way out. And in their feedback, they express gratitude. They will send us e-mails that express such sentiments as, "Hey, you guys have changed my life. I'm so glad I found you. This has been a game changer for me." Those testimonials are a reminder that we are doing the right thing and that we are helping people. My guys on the front lines share with me the expressions of gratitude that they receive, and that's what makes the job worthwhile. People come to us with so much pain on their faces, and when that pain turns to relief, we know that we have done our job.

People don't generally, however, express their gratitude in an online review—after all, who wants to post online that they have been deeply in debt? They don't want to talk about their troubles in public, quite understandably. At one point, as we launched this business, I thought perhaps we could do seminars and explain what we do to dozens of people at a time. But it doesn't work that way. People don't want to show their face; they just want to be a voice on the phone. They want to deal with their obligations, but they want to do so anonymously. And I get that. In this world of Facebook and other social media outlets, there are just not a lot of things that are private anymore.

What keeps each of my financial consultants going, I believe, is the satisfaction of enrolling twenty or thirty new clients a month. It is very rewarding to bring people to the point where the light goes on and they realize, "Okay, I do have a way out of this mess. This is really possible," and they commit to the solution.

We try to under-promise and over-deliver. We do our utmost to turn around the client's situation in the best possible way. We do a lot of work on the front end, well before we get paid. We work as efficiently as possible to take a huge weight off the client's shoulders early on, perhaps within a few months. Our focus is to try to get that first settlement done as quickly as possible to show them that the process does work. That is what motivates people to stay with us. They see that they have settled, for example, a $20,000 debt for half of that or less, and that they can pay that off over three years.

That motivates them to find the money, even if they need to borrow it from relatives.

Once they see that the process works, they are eager to move forward, never before having grasped the true possibilities. Finally, they can see what they stand to gain. Finally they can see that this is not too good to be true. Until they came to us, nobody had explained to them that this could be done. As I mentioned before, sometimes people tell us that they don't want to enroll in a program until they talk it over with their financial advisor. Frankly, people with few assets who are deeply in debt seldom have a financial advisor, but having been one for a number of years, I can say that nobody ever came to me and asked me about these programs—and if they had, I would not have known then what to tell them.

We will explore in the pages ahead the various options open to people in debt. It's not as bad as people imagine. Yes, some creditors may still call. Your record may show late payments and charge-offs. But that is a small price to pay for being able to sleep at night because you know that you have taken concerted action to resolve some highly troubling matters.

CHAPTER 4

OUT OF THE DEBT TRAP

Back in 2002, when we were still running the mortgage company and making some pretty good money, we were always looking for ways to diversify. One day we heard the news that the Environmental Protection Agency regulations were going to force the largest surfboard manufacturer, with 70 percent market share worldwide, to shut down. In short, the EPA changed emission standards and the company would no longer receive pollution credits, so overnight its business model came crashing down.

Both of my partners saw a huge opportunity there. They figured he could go to South America and purchase surfboard blanks— the internal foam shapes on which the resin is applied—at a much cheaper price and import them to meet the demand. They and a translator immediately flew to Argentina to load up as many shipping containers as possible with those blanks and get them back to the

United States. It took three months for the shipment to arrive with one hundred thousand surfboard blanks.

In the meantime, however, another US manufacturer had popped up and quickly retooled its molds to produce surfboard blanks, and it had already claimed a large piece of the market share with the EPA's blessing. The Argentina boards at that point were virtually useless. My partner had a hundred thousand blanks that he could not put to use. Just to get rid of as much of that inventory as possible, he began selling them for thirty or forty cents on the dollar—and fourteen years later, a couple hundred of them remain in storage.

My partners ended up with a debt of roughly $120,000. The deal had been done entirely by taking on unsecured debt on credit cards. Those were the days of easy credit when you could start a business and within six to twelve months have $50,000 to $60,000 available in a credit line. Those days, obviously, are no longer with us. My partner had joined with two others in the endeavor, but their names were not on the books or on the credit line. Therefore, when things went south, he was left holding the bag. He had personally guaranteed the money.

That all happened in 2003 and 2004, when the real estate market was starting to unravel. It was right around the time we were talking about getting into the debt settlement or debt management business. At that point, we had not really heard much about the industry. We had always dealt with people who had very good credit, and debt settlement programs obviously are more of an alternative to bankruptcy. It was hard at first to explain to people why getting into that business made sense.

My partner did his best to service his debt for as long as he could. But when the real estate market turned, and we had to shut the doors of the mortgage company, he was forced to short sell his house and was unable to continue paying on the debt. That's when we saw how quickly some creditors are willing to negotiate.

When you start to go late on your payments by a few months, a lot of creditors will come in and do a spot check of your credit. They are trying to determine whether you are a bankruptcy candidate or whether you are simply staying current on everything else but selectively defaulting on one account, hoping that the creditor at some point will settle with you. In my partner's case, he had about twelve accounts associated with his business, and they all showed up on his personal credit report. It was pretty apparent to creditors that he was in trouble overall.

He started to get the calls, all day long. There is a fine line between harassment and collections, and an automated dialing system can press the limit. Sometimes the calls come hourly, depending on how aggressive a creditor is. Suffice it to say that my partner had a dozen credit lines with three phone numbers attached to each of them. Such calls can be so nonstop and stressful that people just stop answering the phone altogether.

What he found was that as he approached the point of being ninety days late on the accounts, the calls were no longer automated. Real people were calling, and they were leaving messages saying that they would be willing to settle for less than what was owed. Creditors will often write off the account after 120 days and get the tax benefit for doing so. There is a sweet spot between the 90th day and the 120th day in which they will try to work something out and get people on a repayment plan or accept a lump sum settlement.

It surprised us that the creditors would do that. We had never seen that happen. My partner found that the creditors were willing to accept less than half of what was owed. Particularly on accounts where there was any question of whether he was responsible for the charges, those banks would negotiate much faster and for a much lower rate.

By defaulting on all the cards, within 120 days my partner had settled his $120,000 debt for a total of $50,000. His FICO score has since recovered. Once accounts are settled, in most cases they still appear on the credit report. After seven years, you can have them legally removed. Today, his credit is back in the 700s. There has been no long-term impact. The only negative that remains on his credit report is the short sale that he did on his house, which lenders view as similar to a foreclosure. He did keep up the monthly payments after negotiating a lower balance, however—and it is missed payments, not the settlement notice, that do the most damage to a credit report.

The lesson is that there is most certainly a way out of the debt trap. My partner was able to move forward again, and we learned how valuable these programs can be. It was an eye-opener for us and sparked our interest in this business. In fact, we might not even be in this business today if that had not happened to him.

We began to look at how we could spread the word to others— we wanted to find people in similar situations whom we could help out. We knew that my partner could not be the only one out there. In the previous several years of running credit reports, we had seen how people were becoming so heavily leveraged. This was an opportunity to launch a lucrative business that could truly help them.

We both were in finance, with plenty of experience, and yet we had never heard of debt settlement programs. We started to do some research and reached out to the larger companies that did it, and we discovered this large but little-discussed network.

Once we started our new business, we found that the creditors actually liked working with us. They knew that we had the ear of the consumers, who were speaking to us. In most cases, the consumers were willing to put money aside to pay on their debts. The creditors therefore didn't see us as getting in the way of their contractual relationship with the consumer. Instead they saw us as a partner.

WHAT IS DEBT MANAGEMENT?

Debt management is a broad term for the kind of services we provide. We refer to our debt settlement program as debt management, but debt management also includes other programs.

One of these is consumer-credit counseling. In these programs, typically run by nonprofit companies, you are paying back 100 percent of what you owe, but you are doing so at a much lower interest rate that the program has negotiated in advance with the creditors. In many cases, the creditors have sponsored the program because it is a means of getting back all of what is owed, even though the rate is reduced. The creditors have already made their profit, and so long as they get back the original balance, they are fine.

Such programs have a low success rate. Only about 7 to 9 percent of people who enroll in a consumer-credit counseling program will come out of it successfully. However, the advantage is that it does not have a huge negative impact on a person's credit report, although each enrolled account is indicated on the report. Some lenders will treat that the same way they would a Chapter 7 or 13 bankruptcy.

Another option under debt management is debt settlement, and that is primarily what we do. We negotiate reduced balances with each of the creditors. In our case, we guarantee to our clients that we will get them a 50 percent or lower settlement, or basically they are not paying. The way that program works is that by the time consumers come to us, in most cases they have already stopped paying their creditors, so they are already currently late, and the damage is already being done to their credit.

We work with the client to set a budget and look at all his or her creditors and how aggressive each of them is. Then we put together a three-to-four-year program in which the client, rather than pay those creditors, sets aside as much money as possible into an escrow account in the client's name. Once that account has built a substantial enough balance, we will negotiate settlements with each creditor, whether for a lump sum or a series of several payments, in which the creditor is willing to take fifty cents on the dollar.

The debt settlement program does typically result in a negative impact on the credit rating, but again that is because the damage has already been done in the form of late payments, not because of enrollment in the program. In our type of program, we have had an 82 percent success rate since 2010. That is a much higher success rate than for consumer-credit counseling. A lot of those who go into consumer-credit counseling will end up in a debt settlement program at some point.

Yet another form of debt management is a true unsecured consumer loan, where we provide a new loan with a fixed rate and fixed term, and clients know exactly what their monthly payments are each and every month. Typically we are paying off higher-rate credit card debt. So, even if I looked at an apples-to-apples comparison of $25,000 in credit card debt versus $25,000 in one of our debt consolidation loans, the client would still have a lower monthly payment because of how the interest is calculated.

About 20 percent of our business comes from these debt consolidation type of loans. These are people who, by the time we find them, have realized that they potentially could have a problem but have yet to start missing payments, or people who clearly would not be a suitable client for a debt settlement program or bankruptcy of any type. This is for unsecured debt, meaning that it is not tied to a car or a home or anything else. All these debt consolidation programs are for consumer debt, and they don't hurt the FICO score—in fact, the consolidation and closing of old accounts could help the score.

DEALING WITH ROOT CAUSES OF DEBT

However, the people who get a new unsecured loan to consolidate their debt have not really addressed the underlying issue, which tends to be overspending or poor budgeting. A lot of those people will come back to us years later and become a client in our settlement program. Unless the root of the problem is fixed, the new loan is more or less kicking the can down the road. The consolidation loan can keep them going, but at some point they will need to address the reason for the debt.

A debt settlement program does force people to deal with the underlying issues. Everything is cut off, and they lose the ability to get credit, to finance new cars and homes. Therefore, a benefit and byproduct of enrolling in that type of program is that people take a close look at how they can tighten their belts. They see that they have been given one more shot, and they feel motivated to do it right. In essence, they learn how to budget. Perhaps the debt was caused by extraordinary circumstances such as medical problems or divorce, but perhaps it was caused simply by overspending. In any case, learning sound money management skills is a huge asset. That is the client's best hope of emerging in good financial shape.

When we meet with new clients, we can look at the situation and break it down to find out exactly where things stand and the best options for addressing them. It is a very personal decision. It is not uncommon for people to qualify for an unsecured loan and have good credit, yet realize that a job loss or a divorce is imminent and decide that a new loan is not going to help their situation. They may decide that it is better to enroll in a debt settlement program and meet the problem head-on, getting rid of the debt rather than kicking the can again.

We work with our clients to develop a budget that is customized for their unique situation. By taking a close look at how much they are spending and what they are spending it on, we usually can figure out where the issue lies. We get to the root of the problem and look for the hot button that explains how they got themselves into their situation. We work out a reasonable budget for them based on their income and how much they need for living expenses. We cannot force them to adhere to that budget, of course, but we can make sure that they apply as much money as possible toward satisfying the debt.

We aim for the lowest monthly payment possible, perhaps a few hundred dollars a month, but we also consider the nature of each of the creditors and whether they tend to be litigious. We consider the creditor's history and reputation for filing lawsuits. So, if someone has $30,000 in credit card debt and virtually all of that is with one lender, the program is likely to look substantially different than it would for someone who is facing five creditors and owes each $6,000.

We do our best to reassure our clients that the best route to deal with the debt is head-on. We can also reassure them that the fact that they have enrolled in one of our programs will not show up on their credit report. What will show up, again, is the fact that they have made late payments, but the enrollment itself will not become an issue.

RESETTING THE CLOCK

The type of debt that we enroll is primarily unsecured loans, which means that certain types of debt are excluded from a debt management plan, such as mortgages and home equity lines. A home equity line technically is a second mortgage—and that industry virtually disappeared in 2008. If a homeowner continued to make payments on the first mortgage, lenders knew that it would be virtually impossible to foreclose on a second mortgage. The holder of the first mortgage, generally a much larger loan, would have to agree to it. When real estate prices tumbled, those second mortgage companies vanished almost overnight. Since about half of second mortgages were used to consolidate credit card debt, people turned instead to debt management companies such as mine.

In addition, we can help people with the settlement of student loans so long as they are not government issued. They are considered unsecured loans if they are through a bank or other lender. However, personal loans that are held at a credit union can present a challenge. If you have a car loan and a credit card at the same credit union, it can cross collateralize those debts. In other words, if you stop paying on your credit card, you can find your car repossessed. It is important to understand that, and few people do.

Only about 3 percent of accounts enrolled in our program will have some type of legal action taken against them. Sometimes creditors do sue the consumer, seeking a default judgment for wage garnishment. People in debt often stick their heads in the sand and fail to show up for the hearing, and creditors know this. Once they get a court order to attach the consumer's wages, the debt cannot be included in a program such as ours. This is one of the worst things that can happen to people enrolled in our program. If we see that happening, we provide some legal representation and try to settle with that creditor as soon as possible. We don't want creditors to gain that type of leverage over our clients.

Debt management, in short, can reset the clock for consumers struggling with heavy unsecured debt. With expert guidance, they can prevent the problem from ever recurring. Formal debt-management programs are not easy, but they are highly successful for consumers determined to meet the requirements and get out of debt forever. Advisors can help to review the client's personal finances and current budget, and offer expert advice on reducing debt and controlling spending habits. The goal is not just to get the consumer out of the debt trap—it is also to make sure the consumer can stay out of it.

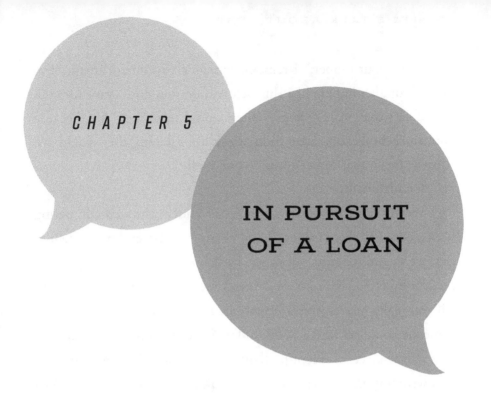

CHAPTER 5

IN PURSUIT
OF A LOAN

t was a time like no other. The entire mortgage lending industry in 2005 seemed to be bubbling over. I remember hiring people who had zero experience to be loan officers, and within a matter of weeks they would be making $15,000 to $20,000 a month. They could buy homes and lease Mercedes.

My wife and a few of her friends had left their jobs waiting tables at places like the California Pizza Kitchen to make that kind of money. I wondered at the time whether there had been any other time in history when someone inexperienced could advance so far so rapidly with virtually no training. All we really needed to teach them was how to look at credit reports.

Some people would come to believe, after doing this for a year or two, that making a couple hundred thousand dollars a year was normal and that they were entitled to that sort of income. In truth, I knew their next job most likely would bring them far, far less, and that they might very well end up back at a pizza joint.

"Save your money," I remember saying to some of them. "I've been through a bubble like this before, and you don't want to be in a terrible situation if it pops." They would tease me. "Just because your stock-brokerage career didn't work out for you," they would say, "doesn't mean that this is going to end badly."

It ended badly.

We would get e-mails every day from lenders who were competing for a piece of all that business. I had to laugh at the lending guidelines that we would see from subprime banks. A borrower could get 100 percent financing with no job, no income verification, and no assets. All you really needed was a heartbeat. Even with a low credit score, someone could get into a $600,000 or $700,000 home and not have to put down a cent, except perhaps to pay for a $400 appraisal. As if that were normal. It is as twisted as thinking you can earn $20,000 a year and wake up to be making $200,000 a year. It was only a matter of time until the great awakening. It was a house of cards. I knew it would come tumbling down.

AN ABOUT-FACE FOR LENDING

The mortgage industry today has gone far in the opposite direction of those heady days when it seemed as if anyone could get a loan. When it ended, it did so very quickly. Banks started to pull loan programs immediately. I would say that 70 percent of the overall market vanished within three or four months.

In essence, what happened was that the loans were packaged up and sold on Wall Street, and that was part of the issue. The loan originators had not been highly trained, and fraud was common. Banks had been looking the other way because they wanted the loan volume. When the fraud came to light, the original bank that underwrote the loan would get it back and have to either service it or figure out how to get it off their books.

The lenders got left holding the bag, and when that happened a few times they really started to tighten up those guidelines. They were running scared, and we are still seeing that today. Lenders are not in a position where they are willing to take much risk, so they tighten up the guidelines almost to the point where the only people who qualify for loans are those who don't need them.

We have been seeing lenders in the nontraditional business of what is known as marketplace lending, or peer-to-peer lending, which has been growing significantly. The peer-to-peer lending space has become an industry in the past several years as banks ceased to lend money to individuals. At this point, it seems to be one of the few sources of unsecured loans. Since peer-to-peer lending is relatively new, we don't yet know what the total outcome will be, or how those loans will perform. Time will tell.

The banks, having once been burned, remain reluctant in a lot of cases to offer loans. If the banks are ever going to get back into the lending game for consumers and small businesses, then credit bureaus will need to change how they evaluate FICO scores. That is already starting to happen. They haven't really reworked the entire FICO program, but lately they have been looking differently at medical collections and collection accounts in general. The collection accounts don't have nearly the same negative impact on credit scores today as they did historically. That should result in more consumers qualifying for loans and should bring more lenders back to the table.

STRICT DOCUMENTATION STANDARDS

Today, all the loans are fully documented with tax returns, paycheck stubs, and verification of assets. It can be particularly tough on self-employed people, who often work their tax situation with write-offs so that their adjusted gross income number is low, and because that is the same number that the banks use, they don't qualify for a loan. The banks request the tax returns directly from the state and federal governments and verify all the information. The situation has gone 180 degrees from where it was.

By 2007, when I was renting a home, the situation had gotten to the point where the real estate agent expected me to provide volumes of information, including three or four years of tax returns, both state and federal, on every business that I had ever owned or had been part of. I remember reminding the agent that I was actually renting the home, not purchasing it. However, that practice has continued to be the standard. If you purchase a house, the lender will go back through two or three years of your checking account and want you to explain any check greater than $1,000, whether you wrote it or deposited it. By comparison, back in the early 2000s you might not have had to verify that you even had a bank account.

The swing toward far more stringent standards has, I believe, slowed down the growth of the real estate market. It has been rebounding fairly well, but I believe the recovery would have been more robust if the lenders had not so strictly limited who could buy a home. It remains that way today: FHA programs of late have been helping, but for the most part it is still very difficult to secure a loan.

CREDIT SCORE MAPPING

The three main credit bureaus—there has been talk about establishing a fourth—have become somewhat more transparent regarding how the system works. Considering how much impact the market meltdowns have had on many people's credit, the bureaus know that they need to let consumers understand the theory behind establishing credit scores. For the first time, people can clearly and easily see what needs to be done to improve their score—and when they do so, they become more attractive to lenders and more likely to obtain loans.

Services are now available that can help people find specific ways to improve their credit score. This is called credit mapping. Let's say you are seeking a mortgage and know that you will need a FICO score of 740 to qualify for a certain type of loan. Credit mapping services will do a "soft" inquiry on your credit report—one that won't hurt your score—and advise you on specific steps that you could take to get there. For example, they might point to five items on your report that, if you attend to them, theoretically would get you above 740.

You can find providers on the Internet, and the cost is about $100. I have used such services myself. In my case, I was advised to take three steps, one of which was to pay down a $5,000 balance that I had on a credit card. The service didn't suggest that I pay it off, but rather that I get it down to $1,200 or so. Paying the card down to zero is not necessarily the best way to help your credit score. The credit mapping service knows that in certain situations, a particular credit bureau may not view a paid-off card as positively as one with a relatively small balance. Once I took the advice, my score rose within two months to above where the service had said it would be.

Credit mapping is a highly valuable service, but it has not been available to the public until recently, and not many people know about it. It can make a huge difference, not only in whether people qualify for a loan but also in saving them significant money on both the rate and the fees. The credit bureaus are all participating in such programs now, so most of the credit bureau websites will have links to trusted entities that they have vetted. If credit mapping had been available back in 2005, I can only imagine how many more loans we could have made.

PROFESSIONAL GUIDANCE

There are online services where you can fill out an application and get back three or four quotes, and those can be a great help in comparing lenders and loans. Such services, such as Bankrate.com, are a good place to start. Look for a loan that has no penalty for prepayment. Also, it is important to compare apples to apples. When you are offered a loan, you should look not just at the interest rate but also at the APR, the annual percentage rate, which takes into consideration all the costs associated with the loan. It will give you a clear and exact understanding of your cost of borrowing over the course of a year, and by looking at the APRs you can more easily compare lenders and loan options.

Be prepared for the documentation that will be required. It does not yet include the kitchen sink, but it might seem like it does. Lenders will want to know about every business you have owned, they will ask for asset statements, and they will want comprehensive financial details from both you and your spouse. Be prepared for a drawn-out process that can seem overwhelming.

Times have changed. In seeking a loan, it helps to obtain expert guidance from someone knowledgeable and experienced. At the moment, it most likely would be hard to find an unsecured loan that would allow you to pay off credit card debt, but a professional who knows what he or she is doing should be able to help you out.

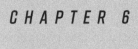

CHAPTER 6

WHY NOT BANKRUPTCY?

The word "bankruptcy" can conjure feelings of dread, as if debtor's prisons still existed and people could be thrown into the clink. Most people, even those of younger generations, still feel the highly negative connotation associated with bankruptcy. They feel as if they have lost, as if they have mismanaged their money and this is the absolute end.

We enroll almost 3,000 clients a month into our debt management program who clearly are just looking to avoid bankruptcy. And most of them indeed would qualify, but bankruptcy becomes public record. It shows up on the credit report for a substantial period of time. Employers now are doing more background checks on people, and bankruptcy is the type of thing that would consistently come up.

We have a number of people in our company who have either filed for bankruptcy or have been through our program, and I believe that the experience gives them insight that they can share with our clients—"Yes, this does work. Yes, there is light at the end of the tunnel."

When it comes to the bankruptcy filing itself, only about 30 percent of the overall credit score is attributed to late payments. The bankruptcy filing itself might result in a loss of 80 to 100 points on the FICO score, so people typically do their utmost to avoid bankruptcy. They try to hold on as long as possible, and they end up with some late and missed payments before actually filing. However, I have seen situations in which people have been able to keep everything current until filing for bankruptcy, and that type of strategy has helped to prevent the destruction of their credit picture.

A FRESH START

Bankruptcy undeniably has that negative impact on the credit score, but it can give people a new start that makes rebuilding much easier. I believe that some people clearly qualify more for a bankruptcy filing than enrollment in a program of debt management or settlement. Although those cases are few and far between, a fresh start with a clean slate might be the best approach for people who are deeply in debt because their child was injured without health insurance, because they faced a major lawsuit, or because of some other financially devastating situation.

One should want to pay one's obligations, and most people do. Millennials and people of younger generations, however, seem to feel somewhat differently. Often their attitude is that they were sold a bill of goods and that it wasn't their fault—that someone else allowed them to get into this position. They have no problem agreeing to pay back a certain percentage of the debt rather than 100 percent of it.

That, of course, is a generalization of the generational views on debt and bankruptcy, but the trend is apparent.

In working with a firm such as ours, people in debt can learn about the options available to them and gain the insight they need for moving forward in the best way possible. Our financial consultants can evaluate people's credit profile and what is going on in their lives that got them into their situation. With that overview and that understanding, they can present the options and talk about the pros and cons of each. The client and the advisor then can make a decision together as to which course of action makes the most sense.

TWO TYPES OF BANKRUPTCY

We do look at the two different types of bankruptcies as possibilities for some clients. The more common type of bankruptcy that you hear about is called a Chapter 7, which is actually wiping the slate clean. By contrast, a Chapter 13 bankruptcy restructures the debt, and a third party who is the bankruptcy trustee makes the determination as to how much the person can afford to pay back. The payments typically can be stretched out, with two to three years the most common period.

Bankruptcies are filed through an attorney. The cost can range from five-hundred dollars to a couple thousand dollars, depending on how much debt is involved and how intricate the situation is. In many cases, people start out with a Chapter 13 bankruptcy but find they can't afford to make the payments, so they end up with a Chapter 7. As far as the negative impact that the filing has on the credit rating, both are about the same. Therefore, the Chapter 7, in which nothing needs to be paid back, is preferable for most people.

A bankruptcy will remain on the credit report for seven years and will remain public record for ten years. Anyone doing a background check will be able to find out about the filing for a decade. After that, you can request that the credit bureaus remove that information so that it is no longer part of your credit profile, but they will just do that automatically.

When you have made the decision to file for bankruptcy, the attorney can walk you through the entire process. This is not something that people should do on their own. There are lawyers who specialize in bankruptcy. They do the filing with the necessary federal agencies. For a Chapter 7 filing, the process takes forty-five days or so. You provide all your credit information, and the attorney goes over a budget with you and makes sure that you are able to qualify. If you make too much money, you simply might not qualify to file for bankruptcy.

Many times when consumers are looking at this process, they have already started to receive collection calls. The bankruptcy process, for both the Chapter 7 and 13, stops those collection calls. That way, the filing relieves a tremendous amount of stress, since those calls can come incessantly. The debt collectors will then try to contact the attorney. Each creditor is notified that the individual has filed for bankruptcy, and at that point the debt collectors are legally required to stop contacting the consumer directly. They must deal with the attorney to figure out whether the filing will be Chapter 13 or 7.

SIDESTEPPING THE STIGMA

The negative stigma of bankruptcy is, in itself, enough reason for many people to seek the alternatives of debt management and settlement. The other major reason, of course, is the long-term blow that bankruptcy delivers to one's credit rating. A lot of lenders operate under guidelines that disqualify someone immediately because of a bankruptcy filing, and that is one reason that we recommend debt management or debt settlement instead for those who qualify. In the last few years, we have started to do more unsecured loans because that often makes the most sense. If someone just needs a temporary loan to get to the next step, and they have some type of income, that can be the way to go.

Again, debt management and settlement plans don't show up anywhere in public record. Through debt settlement, you can accomplish much the same results as in Chapter 13 bankruptcy, but without the long term credit damage. It is not revealed that you have done this. It is quite understandable that people are not exactly eager to offer referrals to businesses such as mine. They are not inclined to go around telling people, "Listen, I did a terrible job at managing my finances, and now I have to start over." Even when something other than doing that poor job led to the debt, people may still harbor feelings of guilt.

CHAPTER 7

FINDING THE RIGHT HELP

You hear a lot of talk about what makes a business successful, and in many instances good timing comes into play. For our firm, it was the passage of credit reform legislation in 2009. The new rules helped to catapult our business, as people saw just what they were up against.

The first measure was the Credit CARD Act (the Credit Card Accountability, Responsibility, and Disclosure Act), signed by President Barack Obama in 2009. A year later, Congress extended the act's reach with the Dodd-Frank Wall Street Reform and Consumer Protection Act, which created an independent federal agency as a consumer watchdog over bank practices.

One of the new provisions required lenders to clearly and prominently indicate on each statement how long it would take for consumers to repay a debt if they made only the minimum payments. No doubt many consumers with credit card debt knew that what they were facing was ugly, but not just how ugly: in effect, the daily compounding interest was putting them on a lifetime repayment plan. The lenders were required to clearly indicate the total cost of that credit. For example, if you have $30,000 on a credit card, you might make the minimum monthly payment of $450 a month, and it would take you 291 months to pay it off, for a total of $212,000 in payments.

In working with new clients, one of the first things that we did was have them gather all their statements and then do a soft inquiry on their credit report. We then walked them through a budget, and we helped them to see that unless they made a change in their spending habits, they would be on a debt treadmill from which they might never escape. It was an eye-opener, I believe, not only for our clients, but also for my financial consultants who worked with them. It cemented their resolve.

The reform legislation also changed underwriting guidelines. We would see situations all the time where a young person just out of college or in their early twenties, who perhaps was a lead clerk at McDonald's, would have $70,000 or $80,000 worth of credit card debt. The lenders had been looking solely at credit score and repayment history. They didn't care so much about income, and they were not so interested in people who paid their credit card bills each month in full. They wanted someone who carried a high balance and then somehow figured out how to juggle things and make the minimum monthly payments. That was the type of people they were looking for.

The reforms led to more of a commonsense type of underwriting, but I know that these companies still don't do any type of income verification, which I find shocking. Other lenders, whether mortgage or auto finance, ask for the most recent pay stubs or for two years of W-2s. We do a lot of unsecured consolidation loans, for which we not only verify income but also look closely at how long the applicant has had his or her job and whether it is in a stable industry. We want to make sure that people are able to pay back the money we lend to them. I think credit card companies need to start taking a good hard look at that, or they are going to end up right back in the same place they got themselves into in 2005 and 2008.

The reform act also stopped the industry from changing interest rates at any time and from using hidden provisions to trigger unjustified fees. The act also limited marketing to college students (although some lenders seem to be getting around that by issuing high-cost debit cards to students). Altogether, the changes have given consumers greater clarity on the terms of credit card offers and protection from unfair practices. In the years since the act's passage, consumers have saved billions of dollars in fees, according to a recent analysis.

Though there still are improvements to be made, the reforms have led to a greater awareness of the credit treadmill that results from making only minimum payments. People are waking up to the need to make major changes or else risk being trapped in debt for decades, or for life.

The credit card reforms were a game changer for us. Never before had all this been spelled out so clearly for consumers, who had simply worked the treadmill without thinking much about the total costs of all those monthly payments. They had focused on whether they could meet the cash flow, figuring that at some point they might make a little more money and be able to pay down the card. When the reform act threw the facts in their face, they woke up. They realized they needed help, or they would never get out from underneath that debt.

That awakening was a win for businesses such as ours. Other new regulations in 2010 helped as well. Until then, attorneys and companies such as ours could charge upfront fees prior to getting a settlement arrangement in place and a payment plan with a reduced interest rate. The Federal Trade Commission invoked telemarketing rules and said, basically, "If you are going to be in this business and help people, then the program needs to be performance based." That, too, was a win for us, because about 65 percent of the industry soon backed away. The change hurt their cash flow, and they didn't see how their business model could continue, considering that they needed to pay for marketing and sales and operations. In effect, I think the change got rid of some of the bad apples in the business, the people who were in it just to make money and not to help people.

When upfront fees were permitted, more than six hundred companies were out there. In the way the payments were structured, it was not uncommon for a consumer to enroll $30,000 worth of debt in the settlement program and pay a fee in the $4,500 range, payable over perhaps nine months. In other words, the consumer would be paying a $500 a month fee. In many cases, that $500 a month went directly to the debt settlement company and didn't go into an escrow account toward immediate payments to creditors. That resulted in a very high volume of losses and default judgments and legal activity.

The overall customer experience today is much different. Today we must show performance, and if we don't perform, we don't get paid. That has put a great deal of responsibility on the company to do things correctly. The Telemarketing Sales Rule has led to a huge change in the industry, and it has been for the better.

A FAR BETTER CUSTOMER EXPERIENCE

A third-party evaluation, commissioned in by the American Fair Credit Council and conducted by forensic accountant Greg J. Regan, compared the debt settlement business before 2010 with the years afterward. It tracked about one-hundred thousand consumers who went through this program, assessing their overall customer experience. It shows that the changes in the industry have clearly created a much better customer experience.

In the old model, it would not be uncommon for us to run into a consumer who had $75,000 in credit card debt and minimum monthly payments of only twelve or fifteen dollars a month. The consumer either figured out a way to continue making those minimum payments, or they went to one of those debt-relief companies that charged them $15,000 to $20,000 in fees. Because the program wasn't underwritten and set up properly, they virtually destroyed their credit and ended up getting sued by each of their creditors.

Often, the creditors would take a spot check of the consumer's rating while the consumer was enrolled in a program. If they saw that the person was delinquent on every account, they would conclude that he or she was headed for the edge and could become a bankruptcy candidate. Creditors figured they should make a settlement offer and try to get as much money as possible before the consumer filed for bankruptcy. The creditors also tried to spot consumers who were doing a selected default, hoping to trigger a settlement. In those cases, the creditor would escalate the legal activity incredibly fast. They would get the consumer into court as quickly as possible, thinking the person was not facing a real hardship and was just trying to weasel out of a portion of the debt.

So, in some cases we saw people who would pay high fees to a settlement company but nonetheless get sued on each account—and lose by default judgment, just like in traffic court, if they failed to respond to the summons. That meant the consumer faced not just the balance of what was owed, but also collection costs and interest. I saw cases where people with relatively good credit came into a program with $75,000 in debt and paid $15,000 or so in fees. Their credit was virtually destroyed in the program, and at the end they owed a whole lot more than $75,000—and they were forced into bankruptcy.

Such experiences gave the debt-relief industry a poor reputation. Before 2010, the industry had a black eye as the word spread about such rip offs. To this day, five years after the credit card reform act was passed, the skepticism lingers. I need to remind people that we are a performance-based company. That is our business model, and that means we don't get paid unless we help people obtain legitimate settlements.

EXPLORING YOUR OPTIONS

People worried about debt might do almost anything to get rid of that debt, and sometimes they make some poor decisions out of desperation. Many companies have tried to make a buck off people's struggles, particularly before the reform act passed. Unscrupulous debt "experts" have been known to crawl out of the shadows.

Consumers must be on guard. Bogus offers are easy to spot. The "deal" will seem too good to be true. You may hear claims that you will be out of debt as soon as you sign and references to some mystery government program.

In many cases, if you do a simple online search for "getting out of debt" or "how to avoid bankruptcy," you'll see a list of a variety of companies. Many of them are lead-generation companies. These are third parties that are searching for prospects and routing them to debt settlement companies for enrollment.

It is important to do your homework. You can go to the website of the American Fair Credit Council, where you will find a code of ethics and guidelines that companies that are AFCC members need to abide by. If a company that you are considering does not follow those rules, you will want to look for one that does.

On the website, you can view a company's Better Business Bureau report. Look at the ratio of the number of complaints to the number of clients, and consider the percentage. For example, a hundred complaints for a company with 275,000 clients is an entirely different picture than a hundred complaints for a company with far fewer clients.

After digging deeply online for any information you can uncover about a company, you should also call it and ask to be sent information, including a copy of the contract. You should have the right to withdraw from the contract after a few days if you decide that proceeding is not in your best interest.

The company that you choose should open an escrow account in your name so that you have total control over it. Some companies will use a model in which monies are commingled in an attorney's escrow account. I believe that is a dangerous practice. If something were to happen to that account or to that attorney, or if a class action lawsuit were to be filed, your success in the program could be in jeopardy. You should not work with a settlement company that commingles funds.

Also, look for companies that have been around for a while. You don't want to get involved with a fly-by-night operation. Look for one of the larger companies out there, and avoid the smaller shops with only five or ten people who are still trying to find their way.

Be cautious when you get cold calls. You may have submitted information online somewhere, and you can never know where it might end up. We are seeing a lot of offshore calls coming from places such as India and the Dominican Republic, where it is much cheaper to set up a call center. Their goal is to find out as much about your situation as possible and transfer you to a company that will try to help you out. Be very hesitant about dealing with any of the overseas entities.

The best companies do not do any form of cold calling. Cold calling is a sign that someone wants to grab a buck and not truly help resolve debt issues, and credible companies seldom use such tactics. Instead, they advertise, and people in a predicament call them, not vice versa. Credible companies do not chase down people who may not be interested.

After you have done your homework and weeded out anyone you suspect could be unscrupulous, what are your basic choices for getting out of debt? We have already looked at a variety of options in earlier chapters. The following is an overview, with more details.

CONSUMER-CREDIT COUNSELING

In addition to its evaluation of the debt settlement business, the Regan report also examined practices of consumer-credit counseling, in which people continue to make the minimum monthly payments on their cards and pay back 100 percent of what they owe, but do so at a much decreased interest rate. Most of the time, the account is closed and can no longer be used, and the consumer is put on a fixed payment term.

Unfortunately, getting such a break often does not do enough to change the consumer's overall financial picture. The success rate is low—in the 5 to 8 percent range—and often people who enter into a consumer-credit counseling program will go on to file for some type of bankruptcy. Chapter 13 bankruptcy actually is similar in some ways to a consumer-credit counseling program, but of course bankruptcy has a long-term impact on credit rating.

Lenders do view consumer-credit counseling in the same way that they view bankruptcy. If someone goes into a program and a lender pulls that person's credit, the report indicates the account that has been enrolled. However, a reputable consumer-credit counseling company will go to the credit bureaus and request that they reinstate the account when someone has graduated from a program and paid off the debt. Basically, that refreshes and updates the credit report to reflect the success of the program.

A consumer-credit counseling company has established relationships with creditors. Let's say you have four accounts of $5,000 each with four lenders. The consumer-credit counseling company will contact each of those entities and let them know that you are facing financial hardship. The company will give them a copy of your budget and serve as a liaison to try to get your interest rates lowered.

Although your accounts will be frozen, and you will no longer be able to charge on those cards, your new interest rate could be as low as 3 percent—or it could be as high as 12 or 15 percent, depending on your original rate. At that point, you continue to make one payment to the consumer-credit counseling company.

The average term of that program is four or five years, and if you are dealing with a reputable entity and can stay the course, it can work out well. For those who can make it through the program, the results can come in that relatively short period, the credit report can be refreshed, and there will be no evidence at all that they ever enrolled in a program.

Potentially, people could do this on their own and contact each of their creditors to say, "I am going through a hardship, and this is my budget." Many of the lenders will have some type of hardship program available so that you need not go to a third party. An interest rate of 17 percent, for example, might be reduced to 6 percent. The process could be a little cheaper for consumers, since they would not be paying a service fee to a consumer credit-counseling company. And even lenders that don't have an in-house program still might be able to offer a referral. That could be a good place to start.

CONSOLIDATION LOAN

A consolidation loan is basically a new loan provided by a third party in which the funds received from the loan will be used to pay off the consumer's existing debt. Our programs are for three or five-year terms, depending on what the client can afford. The loan is for a fixed rate and a fixed term—for example, a new loan at 7 percent with the same monthly payment for forty-eight months, at which time the loan will be paid off, with no possibility that the account will be growing.

Most credit cards compound interest on a daily basis. On a fixed-rate, fixed-term installment loan, the interest is calculated only one day per month. Therefore, a $20,000 debt at 12 percent on a credit card is far different than a $20,000 debt at 12 percent on a fixed-rate installment loan. The amount that you pay will be far less on the latter. In addition, the loans that we offer are typically at a lower interest rate. That provides quite a bit of payment relief. It is not uncommon for someone who was paying $1,200 for each payment to see that drop to $700. As long as they make those $700 payments, they will be totally out of debt by year four.

This will produce no blight on the credit score. In most cases, if you are paying off three or four accounts and replacing that with one loan, it should be a credit-neutral activity. You should not see any type of impact. Once in a while, we see situations where someone might have, say, fifteen creditors, and when we pay off and close all those accounts, there might be a small, near-term negative impact on the credit score. Closing an account can cause a three-to-five-point ding in the score.

We always tell people that unless an annual fee is associated with the account, just pay it down to zero but don't close it. If you keep that account open, there is usually no negative impact. It's when you actually close the account that your score gets dinged slightly, and if you are closing a large number of accounts, those dings can add up.

Besides lowering your interest rate and monthly payment significantly without damaging your credit, a consolidation loan can also have a dramatic psychological effect: No longer are you dancing around trying to pay off ten or fifteen or more bills on time every month. You have one payment to make, and it is significantly lower than what you were paying when you totaled up all those others. You are getting a distinct financial break, but another major benefit is peace of mind.

A consolidation loan is one of the more attractive ways of getting out of debt. It has been very hard traditionally to qualify for this type of loan, and it has been particularly difficult since the economic troubles of 2005 and 2008. Many lenders have stopped offering them. They are wary of any debt that is unsecured, but people with relatively good credit can qualify.

In general, the type of client who enrolls in a consolidation loan program is very different than one who enrolls in consumer credit counseling or debt settlement. A consolidation loan is for a consumer who just needs some temporary help. Such consumers don't need a total restructuring of debt, and they are able to proceed with their credit intact. For those who qualify, it is one of our preferred options.

People who seek a consolidation loan may have had the foresight to realize that something needed to be done, but they still must deal with whatever underlying problem got them into that situation. Perhaps it was poor budgeting and overspending. That is why, in many cases, we will not recommend that someone take out a second mortgage or something similar to pay off debt. It can help with the cash-flow crunch, but it does not address what may be the root issue of overspending. In many cases, people who got consolidation loans may come back to us again for a larger loan once they have racked up those credit cards again. By contrast, debt settlement or consumer credit counseling tends to change behavior, because the accounts are frozen for a while with no opportunity to run them back up.

DEBT SETTLEMENT

Debt management is the overall term that we use to describe debt settlement, consumer-credit counseling, and consolidation loans. Any or all of those can encompass a debt management plan, although we often use the term specifically when referring to settlement.

Settlement is an alternative to bankruptcy, and it is for people who have already missed payments and are overburdened with debt. We take a look at their creditors and underwrite their file with the aim of guaranteeing that we will settle their debts for about fifty cents on the dollar. A $20,000 debt, for example, might be settled for $10,000. The payments, which will be significantly lower, go to an escrow account in their name. They do this for three or four years until they have met the obligation, and they can't use the account during that time.

Meanwhile, once that account builds a sufficient balance, we use it to settle with each of their creditors. That's why it is important to work with a debt settlement company of substantial size. The company needs to have established relationships with those creditors. For example, on a monthly basis, Bank of America, Wells Fargo, and Discover will come in and scrub our books, looking for clients that we have in common. Perhaps one of those entities will find two hundred clients in common and decide to do a bulk settlement with all of them, accepting forty cents on the dollar. Then we contact each of those clients to let them know that the creditor is willing to make a deal—and advise them on whether they should take it, not take it, or wait this one out.

Other than bankruptcy, debt settlement is one of the fastest ways out of debt. However, the credit report will still show the late payments and charge-offs—those don't disappear simply because the client enrolls in the program. Remember, about 30 percent of a credit score is based on payment history, so until all the settlements are fully in place, the damage can continue. In a three- or four-year program, we might not settle with the last creditor until the end of year three. Meanwhile, the original account likely will be charged off, and it could be sold to two or three collection agencies before we have the chance to settle with them. Still, by enrolling in such a program, consumers are well on their way to healing their debt issues.

REFINANCING AND SECOND MORTGAGES

When the real estate crisis began, the lenders who were doing second mortgages and home equity lines of credit—essentially the same thing—basically disappeared. As real estate prices began their steep decline, those lenders pulled their programs immediately. Since those days, we have seen a few lenders jump back into the market, but even now none of them will lend up to 100 percent of a home's value.

Typically, a first mortgage would cover up to about 80 percent of the value, and then the homeowner would be able to get a second mortgage to pay off some unsecured debt. In fact, before the 2008 financial crisis, a few lenders out there would lend up to 125 percent of a home's value. Those loans typically were for people with good credit who were looking to pay off credit cards that they had at a higher interest rate. Those lenders have not returned to the game yet, and the disappearance of those types of programs has led people to turn to more nontraditional options. Our business has benefited by providing sound alternatives for people in need of paying off their debt.

As lenders have been reluctant recently to take as much risk, they have moved away from the concept of allowing consumers to use a home's equity to pay off credit card or other unsecured debt. It has become difficult for homeowners to tap that equity—quite a change from years past, when many people pulled out money every few years as property values rose.

Mostly that has been due to the government's involvement. The government-sponsored enterprises Fannie Mae and Freddie Mac have both been allowing people to borrow up to a higher loan value. This has largely not been the initiative of the individual lender, however, but is resulting from the federal government backing those loans. The support programs seek to keep the machine moving, lest the entire market come screeching to a halt. The officials know that transactions must take place if property values are to return to where they were and if the markets are to build momentum.

We have seen some movement on the private mortgage side, though, as some individual banks are willing to provide 80 percent loan-to-value, or offer programs in which the down payment can be 10 to 15 percent instead of the traditional 20 percent. It remains very difficult for many people to qualify for those types of programs, however.

Even for those who do qualify, it is important to remember that such loans in effect are turning an unsecured debt into a secured one. Does it make sense to convert a credit card debt into a thirty-year loan linked to your home? Loan officers have often told people that refinancing a home is a great way to consolidate debt. Instead, I think doing so just means you are trading unsecured debt for secured debt. In many cases, that debt is then tied to your home, which someone might later try to seize.

You're also turning that debt into a longer-term debt. If you have a thirty-year loan on your home, not only have you just secured that loan with your home, but you have also decided that you are going to pay on it for the next three decades. Homeowners tend to refinance every seven years or so. It is rare, therefore, to run into people who have only ten or fifteen years left on their home loan. Refinancing debt by rolling it into the home loan can make sense from a cash-flow standpoint when the homeowner looks at total monthly out-of-pocket expenditures. However, consider that the loan is now likely to be accruing interest for all those many years.

When you do the numbers on the total cost of borrowing, you get the full picture of why this might not be such a wise move. It's one thing to consider a home-equity line of credit or some other shorter-term obligation to satisfy a temporary need, but I believe in general that refinancing a primary mortgage to pay off a lot of unsecured debt is not the right thing to do.

DEBT INVALIDATION

Some companies practice what is known as debt invalidation, in which they make the claim that the debt does not belong to the individual in question. The aim is to put the responsibility back on the credit card company to prove that the debt does in fact belong to that particular consumer.

It is a legal loophole strategy that rarely works, but it is a strategy that can seem attractive to some consumers. It's basically saying to the creditor, "Hey, that doesn't belong to me, and we're going to make you prove that it does."

The debt-invalidation strategy seeks to make the credit card company go back and pull the original file of the credit card application and establish that the signature is actually the consumer's and that the charges are legitimate. Credit card companies have hundreds of thousands of clients. Requiring them to go back to the original documentation can be quite difficult. In a few instances, the strategy may seem to work, but the creditor usually resurfaces in some way at some point—whether with a collection agency or some other third party.

CAUTION AND DUE DILIGENCE

A cautious strategy is essential when considering ways to get out of debt. Do not share excessive information about your situation when negotiating debt. Volunteering too much information could hurt you more than help you.

This calls for due diligence. Never rush into a deal with a debt settlement firm. You need counseling from credible professionals. You should be particularly cautious when dealing with collection agencies, which will try to extract as much information from you as they can. The original creditors, likewise, will try to be the ones to decide what you can really afford to pay. You are the one who should be making that determination.

A lot of times, the creditors will ask for a personal balance statement or paycheck stubs or whatever they can obtain from you to find out how much money you are making. They are trying to decide whether you are just overspending and whether you have the ability to pay back the debt in a more aggressive fashion. Sometimes people provide the requested information believing that the greater their cooperation, the more lenient the collector will be. It does not work that way. Remember that individual collectors may be paid a commission based on how much money they can extract from the debtor.

Therefore, you should be very careful about volunteering and providing any type of paycheck stubs, W-2s, tax returns, or similar documentation to commission salespeople. The last thing you want to do is give them the control in deciding how much you supposedly can afford. In most cases, when people do that, they end up with a worse deal than they could have gotten by hiring a firm such as ours to go in and negotiate the debt.

In fact, if you know how the game is played, it often is a good strategy to deal with some of the creditors later in the month. Debt collecting is a sales position, and those salespeople have quotas to meet. Later in the month, as they are trying to hit quotas and bench-marks, they may be more apt to give the consumer a somewhat better deal. We find that about 37 percent of all our settlements take place in the last seven days of the month.

In deciding on the best route to take, remember that there are many companies out there that are claiming that they can do a lot of things, and that is why due diligence is so important. Do your homework. You can consult with a number of entities, such as the American Fair Credit Council, that serve as watchdogs of the debt management industry. The AFCC is a good place to start to make sure that the company with which you are dealing is reputable and abiding by FTC rules on how to do business.

As I mentioned earlier, the FTC recently ruled that debt management companies must be performance based—even the models that try to hide behind attorney-client privilege in order to charge upfront fees. You should not be dealing with anyone who is charging an upfront fee or retainer fee before providing services. The services need to be performance based, or what we call "on a contingency basis"—meaning the company doesn't get paid if it doesn't do what it says it will do.

You should be offered a contract that specifies the expectations and the fees, and it should include a three-day right of rescission so that you can opt out if you decide that what you have signed is not in your best interest. Most companies will provide you with an advance copy of the contract so that you can review it prior to enrolling in anything. Steer clear of any company that won't let you do that.

Ask about the company's track record. In many cases, the company will not provide names of clients, but it can provide testimonials about situations the clients have been in, and the results that they got from the company's services. If the company will not provide that to you, or has nothing of that nature, that's an indication that you might want to look elsewhere.

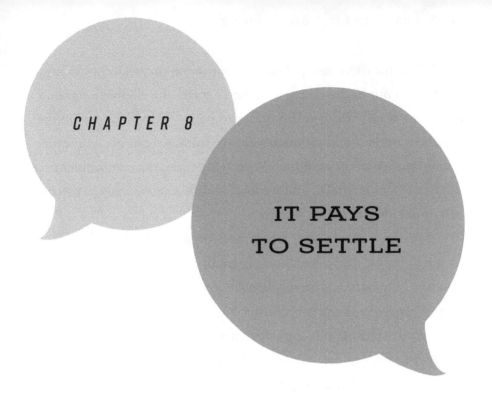

CHAPTER 8

IT PAYS TO SETTLE

n many cases, consumers who are looking for a program to help them get out of debt are already in a delicate state. They may have already started to miss payments, or they are so highly leveraged that they realize they need help.

Typically, once they reach out to us, we run them through a preliminary budget and do a soft pull on their credit report—which, again, is an inquiry that has no negative impact on their credit rating. That allows us to see exactly how much the consumer owes and to whom it is owed. We can see the account balances and the minimum monthly payments.

It is important that we be aware of that information, because some creditors are much more aggressive than others. When we identify such a creditor, one who, in our experience, is more likely to take action, we may move that creditor to the front of the list to be contacted first. We want to deal faster with those who are likely to take legal action the quickest.

Once the client has spoken with one of our financial consultants, we will do our underwriting and then explain the eligible programs. These are usually three-to-five-year programs. We will lay out all the payment options and estimate what we think we can get as a settlement for each of the creditors. We usually make the commitment of fifty cents on the dollar, and we look at different monthly payments that would fit the client's budget.

For those clients who are current on all their bills when they come to us, we take a look at their credit to see whether they could qualify for a loan, and we explain the costs and fees and minimum monthly payments and other terms. However, debt settlement clients typically are already missing payments, and by the time they get to us, they usually are late on almost everything.

They may be receiving creditor phone calls already. We talk to them about how to address those and how to deal with them. We explain that we will reach out to those creditors, letting them know that the client has enrolled in a debt settlement program and that any further correspondence should come directly to us.

EASING THE ANXIETY

Ending the phone calls plays a big role in reducing the stress. When you fill out a credit card application, you are asked for all your phone numbers and perhaps the names and numbers of a few relatives who are not living with you. In many cases, before the account is settled, the creditor may start to reach out to some of those people on the credit application, which clearly can be highly embarrassing.

The debt collector is not supposed to reveal much about how much debt is involved, but nonetheless we have seen some who have told a relative, basically, "Listen, you need to reach out to your friend Bob and let him know that we're looking for him. He owes us $15,000." It is a humiliating scenario, and it can be even more stressful than those nonstop phone calls. In California, creditors can start to make phone calls at eight o'clock in the morning and continue until seven at night.

We can help to put an end to that high anxiety by contacting the creditors after the consumer enrolls in a program. In some cases, that will stop the phone calls, but it really depends on which creditor we are dealing with. Legally, the consumer has signed an agreement with the creditor, and we cannot intervene too much in that direct contractual relationship. However, when accounts are sold off to third-party collection agencies, they are much more willing to deal with us. They tell us that they understand that the client has enrolled in a program and just want to be kept posted about when the money that is set aside in the escrow account will be available for negotiation.

In summary, we start with a full budget analysis and review the client's accounts and credit report. Then we make a recommendation for eligibility into a program. Rather than the consumers making monthly payments to their creditors, they will be paying into a third-party escrow account over which they maintain total control.

Once we negotiate a settlement with the creditor, we call the client and explain the terms. If the client approves, then we contact the creditor and send the money from the escrow account. In some cases, when the consumer does not have sufficient money set aside in the escrow account, we even set up a payment plan, perhaps four or six installments, and then move on to the next creditor. The consumer should be getting a settlement offer every four to six months if the process is going smoothly.

HOW WE MAKE OUR MONEY

On the loan side, we charge an upfront origination fee to secure that loan. Most often the fee is about 3 percentage points of the loan. It can be up to 5 points, depending on the state. There are other fees associated with the loan. We don't participate in any of the interest charged to the consumer. In some cases, if the consumer needs to pay off certain debts to qualify for the loan, we direct the payments directly to those creditors. That way, the consumer becomes eligible and can afford the loan, and at the end of the day is, in fact, using the loan for debt consolidation purposes.

On the settlement side, since it is 100-percent performance based, we get no advance payment. Under our business model, if we enroll, say, 3,000 consumers a month for settlements over four-year time frames, we only get paid every four to six months. We need to make sure that we are doing a great job on customer service and keeping consumers aware of precisely what is going on. Otherwise, we don't make any money.

Once we have performed, then the fee that we charge the consumer varies on a state-by-state basis. On the low end, in states such as Utah, the fee is about 9 percent. On the high end, such as in California, the fee is about 21 percent. That is the percentage of the debt that comes to us as our payment, on top of whatever amount we obtained for the client as a settlement. For example, if the client settles for forty cents on the dollar, the 21 percent fee is added on top of that—so the consumer is paying a total of 61 percent. The savings on the debt is 39 percent, not 60 percent.

A reputable company will convey that essential information to the consumer in a clear and concise manner. There should be no ambiguity about such an important aspect of the settlement arrangement. Nonetheless, a lot of companies will gloss over that part.

Obviously, a fee as high as 21 percent amounts to a considerable sum of money. It reflects the fact that a debt-management company invests a lot of time and effort in dealing with the consumers and creditors and in arranging the settlements. However, with any company, that fee is fully negotiable.

A PROVEN STRATEGY

Debt settlement is a proven debt resolution strategy that helps you get out of debt in a prescribed period of time. As you build up new credit over time, you can improve your credit score. In short, debt settlement lowers your stress level.

The debt settlement firm can contact creditors and work out the terms faster than you could do if you went into the process alone. We can negotiate accounts for multiple clients at the same time and get better deals that way. We do not generally approach the creditor or collection agency to deal with a single account, although sometimes we do so if the agency is very small.

The collection agencies know that we have the ear of numerous clients and that we have money set aside from clients to pay toward the debt. Because of that relationship, we have much greater bargaining power and can negotiate across the board. That is what has enabled us to become one of the largest debt-management agency, with over $6 billion enrolled in our program. We have helped more than three hundred thousand clients get back on their feet.

IMPROVING YOUR CREDIT

Credit scores can be puzzling to many consumers, and it has long been somewhat of a mystery as to how the credit bureaus arrive at them. Your score can vary greatly among the three bureaus. I have often seen people who will have, say, a score of 720 at TransUnion while their Experian score comes in at 640. The difference in the interest rate that you will receive with those scores is huge. And it could spell the difference between getting a loan and not getting a loan, depending on which bureau's report the lender is looking at.

Toward the end of the program, we will help our clients with credit mapping. We look at everything that has taken place in their credit rating during the previous three or four years, or throughout the duration of the program. Then we make recommendations on how they can improve their overall credit score.

It is important to know how the scoring mechanism works and to be aware that you certainly can influence it. Some of the steps can be as easy as sending a letter to a creditor, asking to have an inquiry removed. Perhaps a husband and wife enrolled into a program, and an account belonged solely to the husband, with the wife being simply an authorized signer. The credit bureaus may have recorded that as a delinquent debt on her credit report. Just by sending a letter, the couple can have that negative removed from her credit file forever. Often, there are many little things that we can do to improve on the credit picture, and we offer credit mapping as a free service to anyone who has graduated from one of our programs.

I have examined my own credit score in that way to look for improvements. Credit mapping is a great tool. Someone who is looking for a home loan can get into a much better program with a score of 740 than they can with a score of 720. There are things that you can do to improve your score even within a month or two. For example, as I looked for ways to improve my own score, I had a credit card with a zero balance and a $10,000 spending limit. I found that my score would be better if I instead maintained a $1,400 balance on that card. As odd as it might seem, the credit scoring mechanism gave me a higher score based on my having a 14 percent balance on a card rather than having the card fully paid off. The typical consumer might never imagine that would be the case. It seems logical that if you pay all your debts down to zero, then that is the best your credit score can look. That is not the case.

We recommend to people that they take out a secured credit card about halfway through the program. Doing so will start to create a positive payment history. Since about 30 percent of an individual's credit score is determined by accounts that are currently being used and are being paid on time, it is very important that people coming out of a debt management program start to establish new credit.

They can secure a card for perhaps $500 and then continually use it and pay it down, use it and pay it down. It is important that it is a card that reports to the three major credit bureaus. You can find out the details of various companies on Bankrate.com or other websites. Basically, you send the company the money in advance, and it sends you a credit card. You continue to use that card and pay it off monthly. The limit that the company gives you is simply the amount of money that you are willing to place with it.

After about a year, the company that issued the secured card most likely will take note of the fact that the consumer has demonstrated the ability to make timely monthly payments. At that point, the company is likely to issue that person a new credit card. By making payments on that new card on time, the consumer will now have two positives on his or her credit rating.

In effect, the company really is doing nothing other than lending you your own money—but the big value there is that you are establishing credit on your credit report. We have found that usually within six to nine months of using such a card and paying it off on time each month, you can go back to that lender and apply for an actual credit card. Your new account may have a limit of $1,000 or $750, but as you continue to make all your payments on time, eventually you will be able to apply for more credit. You will be making yourself loan-worthy once again.

IT'S A TEAM EFFORT

We are one of the few debt-management companies that goes through a very detailed underwriting of each file. I believe that is critically important. Someone might not realize what could happen, for example, if he bought his wife's wedding ring from a jeweler with a credit card in which the underlying loan actually was issued by GE Credit Union. If his car loan also happens to be from GE Credit, he could face a repossession if he gets behind on his card payments because he was not aware of the interactions and the repercussions. As I pointed out earlier, I have seen situations in which the credit union will cross collateralize all the accounts that a borrower has with it. If you have both a Visa card and an auto loan, the car might be repossessed if you stop payments on the Visa card—even though the credit card is an unsecured loan. People have been caught by surprise because they simply didn't know that could happen.

With our company on your team, we can provide you with the guidance needed to avoid such situations, because we are aware of the relationships with specific creditors and have seen how those creditors will react. You want to be working with a debt-management company that knows all the ins and outs. You want your negotiator to have enough experience to say, "Listen, this particular bank in the last ninety days has become a very aggressive creditor, so let's deal with it first and foremost so that we don't see any of those accounts going into legal status."

Teamwork requires the efforts of all involved. The consumers need to make sure that they can save what is necessary to make their regular payments after they are accepted into a debt-management program. That might seem obvious, but it is essential: Having arrived at a settlement, will you be able to come up with the negotiated payment?

That is part of the reason we do the underwriting. I hate to use the word "unethical" in referring to a creditor, but we have seen cases where we had, say, a six-month payment plan with a collection agency. We set up an automated ACH withdrawal, and the creditor got the first five payments. However, the sixth payment didn't go through because of something that happened on the creditor's end. Nonetheless, the delayed payment triggered the settlement agreement as void, and the collection agency then tried to recollect on the total dollar amount.

When you are teamed up with an experienced company that knows that such things can happen and how they work, you can make sure that the checks and balances of the system are working in your favor and not lying in wait to trip you up.

The creditors need to be informed that the consumer is in a program and getting counseling, and they should confirm that they are aware of the approval and of the payment terms. That is a responsibility that we typically handle. We notify the creditors about the situation and let them know the account balances and whom to contact if they have questions. We don't want to get in the way of the relationship between the lender and the consumer, but at the same time we do have all the experience and know-how necessary to proceed smoothly. Typically, we take over the negotiations directly with the creditors so that our client no longer has any contact with them at all.

CUTTING UP THE CREDIT CARDS

Once the consumer has finally gotten out of debt, it's a good idea to cut up all those credit cards, except for one—and keeping that in reserve for use in emergencies only.

That is not to say that you should close those accounts, even if you have been blocked from using them. And you want to have that one card open not just for emergencies, but because in some cases you may be required to produce a credit card—for a reservation at a car rental agency, perhaps, or for an airline. You want to keep a card with a small balance that you pay down monthly. That makes the most sense. As for the rest of your cards, I suggest cutting them up so that you never find yourself using them.

Why should you not close those accounts, even though I am recommending that you cut up the cards? One reason is that it may be an account on which you have a good payment history. You will want that history if you plan to use a debt consolidation loan. You will be better off paying that card down to zero than closing the account. However, if the card carries an annual fee, do consider closing the account, since it makes no sense to pay a fee on a card with a zero balance.

Also, as I mentioned before, your credit score will be impacted if you close an account. Closing one card can cost you three to five points, which might not seem so bad, but if you are closing several cards you could quickly inflict substantial damage to your credit rating. It makes more sense to keep those accounts open with as small a balance as possible. It might seem counterintuitive, but the credit score equation takes into consideration the amount of credit you have available if you should need to access it in an emergency. By closing an account, you are raising your credit-to-balance ratio. If you have multiple cards with a zero balance, it could show that you have the ability to access, say, up to $35,000 worth of credit should you need it. And yes, I agree that it seems odd: You would think that paying off all your cards and closing accounts would signal that you have no reliance on access to credit. You would think that you therefore would come across as the best risk, but that is not the case. Few people are aware of that.

For a similar reason, you should not ask for a lower limit on your cards or a cap on the total amount that you can spend. That, too, could potentially have a negative impact on your score, which factors in the amount of your available credit. Someone who has fifteen credit cards with high limits and zero balances on all of them would be considered a much better credit risk than someone who had access only to $20,000 in total.

PAYMENT BY AUTOMATIC DEBIT

The traditional advice for people on a debt settlement plan is that they should set up a bill pay calendar and stick to it faithfully to make sure the payments are sent on time and in full every month. We usually go further than that. Our clients usually set up direct monthly ACHs that will automatically debit the money out of their account. That payment represents the amount of money they are contributing each month to the debt plan.

The payments are like clockwork. Sometimes we set the debits up to take place twice a month for clients who wish to begin paying off their debt more aggressively. We have found that automated payments significantly increase the chances of success for people enrolled in our programs. For that reason, we have come to require it for both loan consolidation and debt settlement. It makes things easier on the consumer, as the payments become a matter of course whether they think about them or not. The fact that these are automatic debits does not in any way impact the credit score, nor does the lender have any knowledge of our requirement. The presumption is that the consumer has decided that this is what is best, which is indeed the case.

As part of the team effort, consumers who are enrolled in a program should review their credit card statements each month to make certain that the negotiated terms are in place, such as the low interest rate and the waived fees. That is extremely important. Anyone who enrolls in debt management will be getting a number of things monthly in the mail. However, we do give our clients the option of having the lenders send those statements and other correspondence directly to us. That makes it easier for us to manage the communications.

RECOVERING AND REBUILDING

The end result for you, the consumer, is that a debt-management program will allow you to recover from the burden of unsecured debt, and you will come out stronger: You will have avoided filing for bankruptcy, which would damage your credit rating for years, and ideally you will have learned some lessons about money management that will serve you well for the rest of your life.

Meanwhile, that old debt will not haunt you—that is, if the process is done correctly, with professional guidance. After completing a debt settlement program, the negotiator will secure a formal letter or agreement from the creditors specifically stating that the old debt is settled and that the case is closed. It is a gratifying moment when you finally have that letter in hand. Again, in most cases, the debt settlement company also will report the satisfaction of the debt to the credit bureaus, with the impact that the account has now been paid in full and closed.

This is a time when you can focus on recovering your financial well-being. You have regained control over your finances, and in time you will be seeing your credit rating improve. The challenge now is to maintain that momentum toward an unencumbered future.

Getting out of debt and staying there is of prime importance. That is what these programs are all about, and the best way to meet that goal is to follow every step of your debt-management action plan as strategized by your negotiator. Do not apply for, or accept, any new loans unless that is permissible under the terms of your debt-management program—and even then, you do not want to take on new debt unless it is absolutely necessary.

The key is to make all your payments on time and to respect and never abuse the privilege of credit. That is crucial. If you fail to do so, the information and advice that you have found on these pages has been all for naught. Rather than building up your credit, you will further damage it.

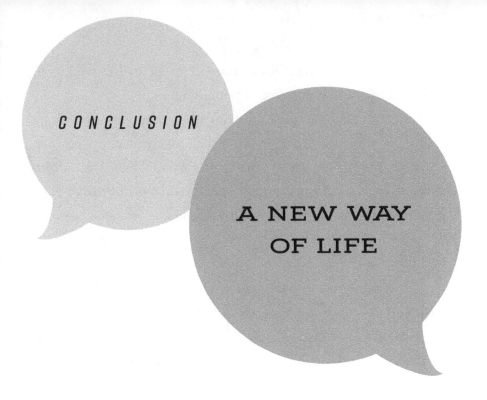

CONCLUSION

A NEW WAY
OF LIFE

I
f you worry that it could take an eternity to regain your credit
worthiness, consider this: Our clients often change the email
address on their credit card statements so that they come directly
to us and we can get in touch with creditors faster while negotiating. Even after our clients have enrolled in the program and have
graduated, those credit card companies still send marketing messages
to those clients—and those emails come to us. I get fifteen to twenty
of them every day. They want those people back. They are trying to
get them back into debt, and so are their competitors.

It is hardly a friendly gesture. They are not forgiving and forget-
ting and welcoming you back into their embrace. They are not your
friends, and they are not acting in your best interest, if they would
see you trapped once again in the cycle of endless payments from
which you have escaped. They are trying to make a dollar. That is
their nature. They are like the drug dealer beckoning to the addict
who just got out of rehab. Don't be fooled: If you were to give in to

temptation when you are still vulnerable, it is highly likely that you would end up back in the same sad situation.

The credit card companies are out to make money. They don't particularly care whether you are struggling with debt, so long as you are paying up. Their favorite clients are those who are in debt and continue to make those minimum monthly payments, laboring away on the treadmill. Unless a major financial windfall comes their way, they will never escape. The system seems structured to make people fail.

We enroll 2,500 to 3,000 clients a month into our program, and as you can imagine we get a lot of mail, and those solicitations to our clients keep coming in, day after day. You can see how profitable these accounts are to the companies because they are willing to extend credit once again to the very individuals who fell short on paying them back the last time. The only reason they would do so would be if they figured they could make money.

Later, after the graduates of our programs regain their ability to get home loans and car loans, they start getting credit card offers in the mail again. Our hope, of course, is that they don't jump right back into situations similar to the ones that got them into trouble in the first place. But the very fact that they are once again attractive to creditors demonstrates that the blow to people's credit is very short term.

Once those accounts get settled and they are back on track and actively rebuilding their credit history, it will not be long before the credit card offers start coming in. That goes to show the mind-set of the credit card companies. They know they are dealing with people who got into financial difficulty, and who took some steps to see what they could do to get out of it, and now the companies are trying to lure them back with offers to get right back into debt.

REGAINING YOUR CONTROL

If you have been in the depths of debt, remember that the goal is to free yourself from it for the rest of your life. A debt-management plan is a great opportunity to reset your spending habits and the way you think about money. It involves more than just figuring out the finances. It's about figuring out your life, where you are going, how you got into that mess, and how you can avoid doing it again.

It is time to transform the need to spend into the need to save. Soon, it can become a way of life as you allocate your resources wisely toward a secure future. It takes strength to ask for help, and I understand that your situation can feel almost paralyzing, but it is not forever. You can rebuild and pull yourself and your family back up to where you deserve to be. You have not failed. You are getting a new start.

You can feel proud that you are doing what is right for yourself and your loved ones. Yes, it can feel overwhelming, and it involves some big decisions, but soon you will see results, and you will be on your way to healing. You don't need to go it alone. You need expert guidance, and in seeking it you are not losing control. Rather, you are regaining it.

Printed in the USA
CPSIA information can be obtained
at www.ICGtesting.com
JSHW012056140824
68134JS00035B/3468